The Second Cross

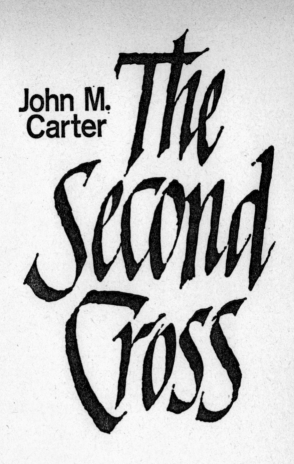

John M. Carter

The Second Cross

Broadman Press/Nashville, Tennessee

This book is personal testimony. It is pub-
lished to enrich the devotional life of the
thoughtful Christian. It should be read in the
light of the author's purpose and of Bible truth.

DEWEY DECIMAL CLASSIFICATION NUMBER: 248.2
Library of Congress catalog card number: 69–14366
Printed in the United States of America
17.7Jy69KSP

Preface

The author's purpose in writing this book is to help many sincere Christians understand a truth on which they have turned their backs, hoping it would go away. But it has not gone away. It survives under many different names—sanctification, baptism of the Holy Spirit, fellowship, spiritual renewal, or spirit-filled life, and others. Regardless of what it is called, no matter is more urgent for the Christian and for the church today than an understanding of and an acceptance of sanctification. Paul stated it: "Be not drunk with wine, wherein is excess; but be filled with the Spirit" (Eph. 5:18).

If the church is to regain the power of the New Testament church it must again have men "full of the Holy Spirit." The church shall surely be strengthened when the requirement for leadership in the church of today is the same as that given for leadership in the early church. "Look ye out among you seven men of honest report, full of the Holy Ghost and wisdom, whom we may appoint over this business" (Acts 6:3). A distinctive requirement for leadership was to be filled with the Spirit.

This book will seek to demonstrate that the higher level of spiritual power attained by many in the early church is still available to the present-day Christian. Moreover, it is the will of God for every man. The Scriptures abound with challenges to the Christian to achieve a higher goal. For those who have received the Spirit the goal is to be *filled* by the Spirit. For those already saved the goal is to be *sanctified*. To those who already believe the goal is to *become disciples*. To those who are already sons of God the goal is to live in fellowship with God.

A new world of truth opened to me the day I lifted one Scripture verse out of the basket which I had labeled for "those out of Christ" and placed it instead in the basket labeled "for the Christian."

I discovered that our Lord was addressing the words, "Seek ye first the kingdom of God, and his righteousness, and all these things shall be added unto you" to Christians rather than to the unsaved. This promise was for me! The truth stood out in bold black capitals as I realized that if I would truly seek *first* the kingdom of God and his righteousness, then I would receive all my necessities.

I write this book (and the one to follow) to aid the Christian in placing the Scriptures in the right "baskets."

There must be no confusion concerning these three baskets of truth: the one labeled for the unsaved, the one for the Christian still living in the desert, and the one labeled for the Christian living in the Promised Land of milk and honey. Truly, the three lands in which a man may live today are symbolized by the three lands in which the children of Israel dwelt.

The first land is the land of Egypt, the land of bondage, a land under the death sentence. This is the symbol of the person without salvation in Christ. The second land is the desert. In this land there is freedom from the death sentence, but it is a land lacking beauty and the bounty of a place flowing with milk and honey.

It is meaningful to realize that the requirement for the

Israelites' escaping the death sentence is the same for people today—faith in the blood of the sacrifice of the Lamb. However, there is an added requirement for entrance into the Promised Land for the Israelites and for people today. What is that? Nothing less than an absolute surrender to God's will and a faith to follow him in possessing a land filled with giants.

Having escaped from the death sentence in Egypt, the Israelites came in their journey to stand at the very gates of the Promised Land of Canaan. Yet the land was denied them until forty years later when their children were ready to make the required surrender to God's leadership. At the very threshold of a great land they stood, hearing God's promise that he would lead them in and aid them in possessing the land. But back, back into the desert they went, because they were unwilling to trust all to God. They were engulfed in unbelief in the power of God to help them against the giants and the walled cities. As they turned away from the Promised Land and trudged back into the desert, they were aware that the requirements for escape from the death sentence and entrance into the land of milk and honey were not the same.

Forty years later when their children stood at the gates of the Promised Land the giants were still there. The walls were probably even higher and more impregnable than before. No doubt the weapons of the enemy were also more effective. Nevertheless, the children of Israel did go into the Promised Land and possessed it under God's power. The difference that brought victory out of defeat was a surrender of self—a willingness to seek *first* the kingdom of God. Their fathers had been unwilling to surrender.

In this journey from Egypt to the Promised Land the Israelites had shared in the experience of two deaths: the death of the lamb for their deliverance from the death sentence and now the death of self, which gave them the power to enter and possess the Promised Land. The reality of these two deaths should not be strange to any Christian today, because they are the two pictures already portrayed in his baptism. "Therefore we are buried with him by baptism into death: that like as Christ was raised up from the dead by the glory of the Father, even so we also should walk in newness of life" (Rom. 6:4).

The same truth is portrayed in the Lord's Supper. As we partake, we are repeatedly reminded of the death of Christ. In this act as believers we confess our faith in the sacrifice of another for our deliverance, and we also commit ourselves to testify to this truth to one another and to all the world until he comes.

Recently I saw a globe of the world which would not turn. Having come loose at one pivot, it hung at a crazy angle. It could help no one, for it offered only a perverted view of the world. When Christianity comes "loose" and is severed from either of its pivots—the death of Christ or the death of the Christian (self-surrender)—it can only offer to the world a perverted view without meaning or help.

Today it appears that Christianity, while becoming more securely fastened at the pivot of the death of self for others, is coming loose at the other pivot—the death of Christ on the cross.

It is our purpose in this book to gather the Scriptures related to the death of self and to point the way to the possession of a land flowing with milk and honey. These

Scriptures are many and will overflow our basket. They will surely reveal God's good, perfect, and acceptable will, for he is saying to the Christian today as he did to Moses: "I have . . . seen the affliction of my people. I will bring them out into a good land, a land flowing with milk and honey" (cf. Ex. 3:7–8).

JOHN M. CARTER

To my wife, June,

whose constant understanding and encouragement,
whose practice of the principles taught in this book,
and whose life has spiritually blessed
the lives of many as she turned them
to the Master,
I dedicate this book

Contents

1.
Spirit-filled

Robert Jones, a Negro sentenced to electrocution, was converted and filled with the Spirit.

The first night he was in prison, the chaplain said one of the hardened criminals brought to his cell was converted. Three more criminals were converted the next night. And the last night every prisoner who crowded into Robert's cell turned to Jesus Christ as Saviour.

As Robert took his seat in the electric chair he said he hoped all those present would repent and go where he was going. Seeing the sons of the man he had killed, he asked their forgiveness. Then he told them he was not the same man who had killed their father.[1]

Being filled with the Spirit always creates a new man, even out of most unlikely material. In order to understand the impact of Paul's plea to be filled with the Holy Spirit several facts must be taken into account. First, the plea that Paul makes is to people "in Christ." These believers had already received the Holy Spirit. Like the children of Israel they had already escaped the death sentence by faith in what Christ had done. However, another step is requested.

These Christians found, as did the Israelites, that what was required to enter the Promised Land (or to be filled with the Spirit) was different from what was required in escaping Egypt and the death sentence.

From Genesis to Revelation there are two themes: (1) salvation through the blood of Christ and (2) consecration through the infilling of the Holy Spirit. Without the former there is no eternal life. Without the latter, there is no Christian joy, no power for God, no life of service, no fellowship with the Lord, no assurance of salvation, and no promise of answered prayer.

Today's Christian could be compared to the hosts of Israelites as they came out of Egypt. They were redeemed. They had fled the land of death, but at Kadesh-barnea they refused to follow God's leading into the Promised Land. The Christian today also has found refuge from the death sentence because of the blood of the Lamb, but like the Israelites of old, facing a Promised Land, they have turned back into the desert. Of all the group who came out of Egypt only Caleb and Joshua lived to see the fulfilment of God's promises. Why? They were the only ones who made an absolute surrender and were willing to follow without reservations the leadership of the Lord as he led them into a land filled with giants.

Paul's term, "being filled with the Spirit," is the same experience as of those entering the Promised Land had after salvation. Frequently the New Testament refers to people wholly surrendered to the Lord in the words, "They were full of the Holy Spirit."

What is meant by being "filled with the Spirit"? An experience from my boyhood may illustrate this. On our farm was a spring which had water only during the rainy season. On my first visit to it one fall I found it filled with water, sticks, stone, leaves and even a frog. It was not filled with water, for it had both water and other things as well. Not until these were removed could it be said of the spring that it was *filled with water*. This truth is applicable to a Christian's life as well. The Holy Spirit can only fill the life emptied of other things.

Still another way to describe the "filling of the Spirit" is to observe the effect he has upon the lives of those who invite him to rule. So evident was this filling with the Spirit that the early Christians were thought to be drunk (Acts 2:13). Paul also recognized that the filling of the Holy Spirit has the same effect, for he wrote, "Be not drunk with wine wherein, is excess, but be filled with the Spirit" (Eph. 5:18). His parallel is a strong one, for he is saying that as wine possesses and dominates the drinker, so must the Holy Spirit possess and dominate the believer in whom he dwells. In the eyes of the world these early Christians acted very strangely. They were speaking with boldness, defying the authorities, willing to accept persecution, imprisonment, and even death. They talked of a man who had been raised from the dead. Their actions were so bold and unusual they were thought to be drunk. Not only were those who experienced Pentecost so changed, but Paul expected the filling of the Spirit to produce similar changes in his day. Like a drunk man he would be so obsessed by a power outside himself that he would not care what other men might think.

Sometime ago I visited Solomon's quarries beneath Jerusalem where huge blocks of stone had been blasted from solid rock before the days of dynamite. When the guide

explained that this tremendous power had been exerted by
small wooden pegs driven into holes, it seemed incredible
until we learned of their secret. The wooden pegs were
driven into the hole and then soaked in water until they
were able to break asunder the rocks. As the water filled
this piece of wood and gave it a power far beyond that of
wood, so the Holy Spirit will fill a life. A new power will
come in, and that which before was impossible can be
accomplished.

What is this higher plane of Christian living? How can it
be attained? We will attempt to answer these questions by
calling attention to certain truths stressed repeatedly in the
Scriptures.

1. Being filled with the Spirit is not a level of Christian experience held by every Christian.

2. It is an established fact that not only at Pentecost, and
in Paul's day, but also today men who have already accepted Christ (and received the Holy Spirit) have later
been filled with the Spirit.

3. In this experience of filling men, the Holy Spirit accomplishes a third mission assigned to him. This mission is
performed in equipping men to reveal Christ to others. One
mission of the Holy Spirit is leading men to Christ. Another
mission is sealing men for Christ until he comes (Eph.
1:13). The Holy Spirit has no office except in relation to
Christ. All work of the Holy Spirit in men will result in
Christ's being magnified. Any work claimed to be of the
Holy Spirit that gives prominence to anything equal to that
prominence given Christ should be rejected as other than
the work of the Holy Spirit.

4. This experience always gave men special powers and

prepared them for superior service—not superior standing. This was a requirement for deaconship in the early church, for they were instructed to select from their number not the most popular or most wealthy but "men filled with the Holy Spirit" (see Acts 6:3).

5. This experience of the infilling of the Holy Spirit sometimes involves a phenomenal experience, but often does not. This was true in the first century as well as the twentieth. This is not because God gives men different gifts, but because men react to gifts according to their own individual emotional dispositions. An experience is determined by two factors: the happening itself and the individual's reaction to it. Caution must be used in stressing any particular experience, either at salvation or the experience of being filled with the Spirit.

It is dangerous to lead men to expect a certain experience that is dependent upon two such variable factors as personal background and emotional patterns. On the other hand, it is just as erroneous for those who do not have an epochal experience to doubt the validity of another's experience, however phenomenal. Often it is regrettable that the experience is proclaimed louder than the change in a person's life resulting from this experience. It never seemed to bother Peter that he did not see a light, as did Paul. A study of the Bible reveals that Paul never calls attention to, or places emphasis upon, this seeing of the light on the Damascus road, except in relating it along with his conversion and other events of his life.

A phenomenal life outweighs a phenomenal *experience*. The constant factor in being filled with the Spirit was not a phenomenal experience but a new power in revealing Christ.

Many who have no peer in this respect never had a phenomenal experience.

Some of my friends will rejoice that I have learned part of the truth concerning the "baptism of the Holy Spirit." I, too, rejoice that they have found part of the truth. Now we must ask, "Where do we go from here?" The most important question facing one led by the Spirit should be how to help others find the way.

It is inconceivable and unacceptable to me that God would leave any doubt concerning the steps to the realization of the state of being filled by the Spirit. To be sure, God did not leave any uncertainty concerning the road to be taken in realizing this experience—an experience so important that its realization is God's desire for all men. And not until its realization comes to men will they be empowered for special service. God would not leave it unmarked.

Why then are some men searching for this way with all their hearts and yet are not finding it? The fault is not with God, but with man. Two errors being made by men today are confusing seekers and hindering them in their search for the realization of God's will in their lives. The road leading to the Spirit-filled life, though crowded with seekers, is marked by many confusing and conflicting signs, pointing in several directions and all purporting to guide one to his goal. Many travelers following these signs do reach their destination, but they arrive from several directions after having followed one of the many marked detours. These detours are not of God's making, for he would have everyone find his fulness of joy. His truth is not shrouded in mystery to be discovered by only a few. His goal is that every man should know him and his power.

The second error some have made is overemphasis of their own personal experience when they reached their destination—the Spirit-filled life. To illustrate, an artist going abroad would find his interest centered in the museums and art galleries. These are the experiences he would relate upon returning home. On the other hand, for those to whom art is not so important these things would have little meaning. Thus, to them the artist's description of what he had found would be neither meaningful nor understandable. To describe a place from the standpoint of what it means to one personally is often so inadequate a description, and so unlike what another will find, there is little recognition of it.

There are, however, certain landmarks that are always found by those who attain the Spirit-filled life. These are the fruits of the Spirit. Paul describes them: "The fruit of the Spirit is love, joy, peace, patience, kindness, goodness, faithfulness, gentleness, self-control; against such there is no law" (Gal. 5:22, RSV). Unless one finds these fruits of the Spirit he has not discovered the good land to which God would lead him. Among the lives who have touched mine I know of none more Spirit-filled than Lucrecia Izquierdo.

Some years ago a group of Cuban students came to study at Campbellsville College. As we entertained them in the president's home at a reception, we were indelibly impressed by the spokesman of the group as she expressed thanks. From that moment our lives became entwined. Knowing she was not a Christian, my wife invited her to visit us for Bible study. A short time later in our living room the two knelt by the sofa and Lucrecia became a child of God. A song we sang, "Now I Belong to Jesus," became very precious to her.

After her escape from Communist Cuba she began teaching in Miami. Then came several "wilderness" years when she stopped reading God's Word and witnessing. In fact, she went back to the Catholic Church. In the summer of 1967, our prayers were answered when she wrote that she had found joy again in Jesus.

Since Lucrecia wrote this letter she has led to the Saviour her godmother; Esther, the sister of the godmother (sixty-seven years old); her niece, Alina, sixteen years old; and an Intermediate boy in her Sunday School class in the Flagler Avenue Baptist Church in Miami. Her Christian witness is daily in the school where she exhibits the love of Christ. In January, 1968, she received her Master's Degree from the University of Miami. But even higher than that is her "degree" in living the Spirit-filled life.

Notes

1. From E. Stanley Jones, *In Christ* (New York: Abingdon Press, 1961), p. 376. Used by permission.

2.

Questions Concerning the Spirit-filled Life

Concerning the Spirit-filled life, there are many additional questions. Although these questions could not be answered in detail without departing from the particular emphases of the remainder of the book, this chapter will seek to answer those most frequently asked.

1. What is the difference between the work of the Holy Spirit in the believer at salvation and a later experience in which the believer is filled by the Spirit?

At both experiences one must be surrendered unconditionally before the will of God can be done.

At both experiences the Holy Spirit fills to capacity the vessel yielded to him. In both cases this is *all*.

At the second surrender and accompanying infilling of the Spirit "the all" may be much more than "the all at salvation." The reason for this is that the second surrender often comes at a time when the believer may more fully realize through the Scripture and leadership of the Holy Spirit that God is actually requesting more from him than he had fully realized at his first experience. Also his own spiritual growth could well result in bringing about the opening up of an additional area of service to which he now needs to commit himself. The experience in each case follows a committal to the prayer, "Thy will be done."

2. Do all Christians need a filling of the Holy Spirit after salvation and apart from the experience at salvation?

Theoretically there probably could be a situation in which there would be no need for another filling by the Spirit. This could be true if the Christian realized at salvation that "all" included both what he knew to surrender then and what would be revealed to him later. A good test for a Christian in determining whether he has lived up to his commitment would be to ask himself whether he has consistently followed the claim of God instead of following his own desires of self-gratification. If one can pass the above test, he is still filled with the Spirit. (Both God and nature abhor a vacuum). However, if after salvation a believer allows self to have priority in his life, he can only be filled again by the Spirit as he dethrones self and gives God right-of-way in his life.

3. Is it possible that a Christian might need even a third or fourth filling of the Spirit?

The determining factor as to whether a Christian needs to be filled by the Spirit at any particular time is whether or not he can at that time pray with all sincerity, *"Thy kingdom come. Thy will be done."* Unless a Christian's first concern is that God's kingdom should come on earth and that God's will should be accomplished in his life in trying to bring this to pass, he is not filled with the Spirit. Paul wrote, "Be filled with the Spirit." A personal inventory might convince one he needs more than a second filling of the Spirit.

4. Are there only two spiritual levels taught in the Bible?

This might be answered by using a parallel. Let us think of a two-story house. In approaching the second floor there are steps and perhaps landings on which one may pause. These steps and landings are only important because they lead one to the top. But each one attained brings the climber to a new level. However, not until he reaches the second floor should the climb end. Steps, stairways, and landings are no place to live. In this book we have not dealt with these steps and landings, but have only emphasized the top floor and the blessings and comforts to be found there. The purpose of this book in helping men know God's will would not be advanced by dignifying the steps and landings and granting to them a place of consideration equal to that of the Spirit-filled life.

One might point to the diminishing size of the group as the sacrifice becomes greater. On the Mount of Olives at Bethany there were *five hundred* who saw the risen Lord ascend to heaven. In the upper room at Pentecost there were *one hundred and twenty* praying. On the preaching mission *seventy* went out, two by two. Only *twelve* went with him everywhere. Of these only *three* shared his glory at the transfiguration, and only *one* lay on his bosom at the Last Supper. Only *one* stayed with him through the trial. Only *one* was given care of his mother. Only *one* was inspired to write the book of Revelation. The Bible refers to this one as John, the disciple whom Jesus loved in a special way.

5. Can a common ground be found on which we can agree that there is this higher level of spiritual experience?

We believe that it can be found. On two major points

already there is substantial, if not full, agreement. First, we agree on the reality of the higher level, and all have a desire, who have already realized it, to help others reach it also. Second, there is substantial agreement by all that the only door opening onto this plateau is through absolute surrender of self to the will of God.

Our differences are not over the reality of the door to the plateau, but in *what fruits will be found there*. For example, there is a disagreement on whether one of the fruits or gifts to be found there is the gift of tongues. Whether one believes or denies that speaking in tongues is a fruit of this plane should not really become a barrier between Christians filled by the Spirit. Tongues are at best only *one* of the *many* fruits found on the heights. Either the presence or the absence of tongues upon achievement of the goal does not merit the concern that it is causing in many circles today. Are we not at this point like two attendants in a gas station? A tourist had stopped at the station to inquire directions to a resort. As the attendant started to reply a bystander interrupted by commenting on how terrible the food was. At this point the attendant took issue with him and a heated argument developed.

As the tourist, who was a Spirit-filled Christian, drove away with his question unanswered he remarked to his friend, "Those two men remind me of some of our Christians today. Sometimes we argue so heatedly over what one will find in the Spirit-filled life that we forget that the most important factor is to direct them to it." Really the presence or absence of one fruit in a land that abounds with so many fruits is relatively unimportant, when compared to the importance of helping others to find their way there.

Is it not the part of wisdom and would it not promote the cause of Christ by joining as one to proclaim to the world in one voice that which we all believe, rather than sounding off in many confusing voices, thus magnifying our differences? We may all be surprised at how near the truth others have come. Most Christians already agree on the "majors" of the Spirit-filled life. Differences are over the minors. Can we not join together in preaching in one voice our common beliefs? Can we not join in urging *the need* today for Christians to be filled by the Spirit? We can join in *pointing out the way,* which when summed up is always through *absolute surrender* to him, that his kingdom might come and his will be done. Can we not agree that each of us not only has the right to enjoy but must also respect the right of others to enjoy the fruits found on this plane? Can we not also accept the fact that men may even find different fruits there? These fruits, we must remember, are the gifts of God. And in God's wisdom he grants to man gifts not only on the basis of his particular need but also on man's capacity to receive.

"Now you are the body of Christ and individually members of it. And God has appointed in the church first apostles, second prophets, third teachers, then workers of miracles, then healers, helpers, administrators, speakers in various kinds of tongues. Are all apostles? Are all prophets? . . . Do all possess gifts of healing? Do all speak with tongues? Do all interpret? But earnestly desire the higher gifts. And I will show you a still more excellent way. If I speak in the tongues of men and of angels, but have not love, I am a noisy gong or a clanging cymbal" (1 Cor. 12:27 to 13:1, RSV). For the sake of others and for the cause of Christ, it is urgent that Christians spend *more effort* helping others to arrive on this spiritual plateau and *less effort* arguing over the fruits that one will find when he arrives. The present confusing, unintelligible, and often contradictory signs erected by various groups are neither the will of God, nor do they provide help to the one making the journey. The present increasing activity of different groups gathering by the highway and frantically waving contradictory signs is incompatible with the action of Spirit-filled men. The will of God for peace on earth and goodwill among men cannot be found by the man seeking it by becoming another member of a group who themselves have not found that peace.

Whatever spiritual heights a man has reached, he has not yet come into the land to which the Holy Spirit would lead him unless he has found joy and peace. "The fruit of the Spirit is love, joy, peace, longsuffering, gentleness, goodness, faith" (Gal. 5:22). These are the fruits of the Spirit. Paul reminds us also, "If we live in the Spirit, let us also walk in the Spirit. Let us not be desirous of vain glory, provoking one another, envying one another" (vv. 25–26).

3.

Sanctification

When General William Booth, founder of the Salvation Army, was asked what had been the secret of his success, he replied: "I will tell you the secret—God has had all there was of me. There have been men with greater brains than I, men with greater opportunities than I, but from the day I got the poor of London on my heart, and a vision of what Jesus Christ could do for them, I made up my mind that God should have all of William Booth there was: and if anything has been achieved, it is because God has all the adoration of my heart, all the power of my will, and all the influence of my life."

Here was a man who was sanctified, completely set apart, whose supreme desire was to do the will of God. No claim of the world upon him could sway him from his decision to follow fully in the Master's steps.

In 1 Thessalonians Paul is writing to the Christians and declaring unto them, "This is the will of God, even your sanctification." No doctrine is more misunderstood than this one. Some have misinterpreted sanctification to mean "make sinless." If this is true, then one should be able to substitute these words for "sanctify." But when we substitute the word "sinless" for sanctify, we find ourselves in difficulty, for in John 17:19 our Lord said, "For their sakes I sanctify myself." If we equate the word "make sinless" with sanctify, then Christ was saying, "I make myself sinless," but he was not saying that. He was never a sinner who needed to be made sinless. Certainly in this instance it is quite evident that the word "sanctify" does not mean "make sinless."

Another use of the word "sanctify" is found in 1 Corinthians 7:14. If sanctify could be translated "make sinless," then it would have to be admitted that a wife who is a believer could make her husband, an unbeliever, sinless. In such a case we would have the unbelieving husband made sinless by the wife. Such a teaching would be contradictory to every teaching of God, and to his very nature. The passage states plainly that the sanctified husband is not even saved, but the wife is encouraged to continue living with him that he might be saved. These two references, as well as others in the Bible, demonstrate that the word "sanctify" cannot be translated "make sinless."

On the other hand, there are some people today who hold an equally erroneous view—that sanctification does not have any special meaning for today. In fact, one is often led to say that the way sanctification is erroneously taught and practiced by this group is often better than the way it is ignored by other groups.

What is the meaning of sanctify? When one substitutes the words "set apart" for the word "sanctify" then many Scriptures heretofore meaningless and confusing reveal great truth. For example, when Christ said, "For their sakes

I sanctify myself," he was referring to setting himself apart to die on a cross for them. In 1 Corinthians we noted previously Paul's reference to the unbelieving husband's being sanctified by the wife. He was simply stating that this husband was set apart from all other men for his wife.

Look also at Hebrews 13:12, where it is stated of Jesus that he sanctified the people with his own blood. He set them apart from the rest of the world to be his own. Or look at 2 Timothy 2:21, "If a man therefore purge himself from these, he shall be a vessel unto honour, sanctified, and meet for the master's use, and prepared unto every good work." The reference suggests cleanliness, separation for use.

Various groups of Christians who emphasize sanctification have recognized the truth, often neglected by so many, that God desires more than just salvation in the life of a believer. Did not Paul write, "This is the will of God, even your sanctification"? The error has come in their declaration that sanctification is a state of sinless perfection. But God emphasizes the truth as "set apartness" for service. The stress of the Bible is on the positive rather than on the negative. There will be a separation from sin, as well as a love outreach to the world as God's instrument.

In order to understand sanctification, every Christian should become acquainted with at least two phases of sanctification. The first is sanctification by the blood of Christ (2 Thess. 2:13). The second is sanctification by the Spirit for service. The first sanctification is the act of God in separating man from the lost and bringing him into the congregation of the redeemed. The second sanctification is the act of God in separating man out of the congregation of the redeemed and calling him into special service. This second sanctification is not the result of the sacrifice of Christ which has already sanctified man from the lost. It is the result of the sacrifice of self which God wills in setting him apart and preparing him for service.

To the Christian Paul writes: "If a man . . . purge himself . . . , he shall be a vessel unto honour, sanctified, and meet, for the master's use." Only by the dethronement of the cares of this world can sanctification be attained. In the parable of the sower our Lord points out the tragic situation of the hearer whose greatest concern was the cares of this world and whose life thus ended in barrenness. "As for what fell among the thorns, they are those who hear, but as they go on their way they are choked by the cares and riches and pleasures of life, and their fruit does not mature" (Luke 8:14, RSV).

Sanctification is the result of both man's dethronement of self and God's enthronement in him of the Holy Spirit. Without the giving of self man is like a pipe, flushed and cleansed, but not filled with the life-giving waters. But when sanctification and filling with the Spirit takes place the pipes are filled.

Consider this.

Confronting the Christian on this great venture of sanctification are giants just as truly as the Israelites of old met them. They, too, had been sanctified by the blood of the Lamb. The good land lay before them, but they could not see it for the giants. Are today's Christians any different? Like their forebears they assume they must fight the giants in their own strength. Like their forebears they have no faith in the might and power of our God to conquer and to deliver. If today's Christian could only realize that his battle is the surrender of self God would then take care of the giants.

Sanctification is a requirement, if one is to be ready for the Master's use. Just as a man cannot use a hoe or a hammer while another's hand is upon it, God cannot use the Christian unless he is set apart for God's will to be done through him.

Throughout the Bible this truth is repeated. Romans 12:1–2 reminds us anew that we are to present our bodies a living sacrifice in order that God may prove what is his good, perfect, and acceptable will. The powerlessness of many Christians today is due to the fact that they are not set apart from the world for service. The cares of the world, the deceitfulness of riches, and the desire for other things is the ruling passion of this age. Our Lord's prayer for his children is that they might learn his truth and through it become sanctified for his service. "Sanctify them through thy truth: thy word is truth" (John 17:17). The call here is to a separation from the world for his service. Is this not the same as the call of the Master to discipleship—forsaking all and following him?

In the Old Testament when the Israelites stood for the first time at the doors of the Promised Land, God promised to do great things among them if they would separate themselves from the ties of the old life. They heard Joshua say, "Sanctify yourselves [separate yourselves]: for tomorrow the Lord will do wonders among you" (3:5). Because of their unwillingness to leave the fleshpots of Egypt they turned back into the wilderness. Forty years later their children would stand there again.

We stand today as they did, saved by the sacrifice of

Christ. The door into the "Promised Land" is also before us. He promises to do great things among us if we choose to enter. But the way back into the desert is also open.

Christians too are looking into the tomorrow and praying for great things, but God's Word comes as clearly and imperatively as to the Israelites, "Sanctify yourselves," and tomorrow God will do great things among you. Too many Christians, however, are unwilling to pay the price of consecration that God might do great things through them.

In World War II two brothers were on the same battle front. During an attack one of them was shot down, and unknown to his brother was left on the battlefield as a retreat was made. Upon reaching the trenches Tom learned of his brother's injury and started to return to the field of battle for him. His comrades warned him of the folly of it. His captain said, "You can't go." He replied, "Captain, I am going, even if you shoot me." Out on the battlefield he went, only to find his brother dying. He returned and the comrades greeted him with these words, "Tom, you shouldn't have gone."

Tears filled his eyes as he said, "Fellows, you don't understand. You see, I just had to go. Just before he died he looked up and saw me and said, " 'Tom, I knew you would come.' Can't you see, fellows, I just had to go. He expected me."

Many are counting on us. May we be as willing to pay the price that we may claim the promise, "Sanctify yourselves," and tomorrow God will do great things among you.

4.

Fellowship

Another hallmark of the Spirit-filled believer is his fellowship with God.

For centuries the wealth of knowledge contained in the ancient writings of the Egyptians was hidden from the world. But in 1822, when Champollion deciphered the Rosetta Stone the key was found that unlocked the treasures of ancient Egypt. There is also a key that alone can unlock the treasury that holds many of God's greatest revelations for man. It is a simple key, but one which few have turned. This little key, which can unlock so much, is found in these two verses in the First Epistle of John.

"Beloved, now are we the sons of God" (3:2), but "that which we have seen and heard declare we unto you that ye also may have fellowship (1:3). A new world of understanding can open to the man who accepts the truth John reveals here, for he states that though you have attained sonship, the journey is not finished. There is a level higher up, a place where one can not only know *sonship* with God, but actually have *fellowship* with him. John leaves no doubt that those to whom he is writing have already attained the first level. In 2:1 he calls them children. In 3:1 he calls them sons of God. In 5:13 he calls them believers. For them the first level had been reached.

The second level is yet to be gained. It is a plateau higher up, a place of fellowship with God. "Truly our fellowship is with the Father and with his Son Jesus Christ" (1:3). It is a place of *joy*. "These things write we unto you, that your joy may be full" (v. 4). John could write of this, for he had already experienced it. "That which we have seen and heard declare we unto you, that ye also may have fellowship with us" (v. 3). This is a level yet to be reached by those who have already become sons, for to those John writes, "Beloved, now are we the sons of God" (3:2) and these things "write I unto you that ye also may have fellowship" (1:3).

In order to show the difference between relationship and fellowship, we use an illustration from family life. Any father or mother will readily understand, because they know that parents and children (relationship) are not always at peace (fellowship) with one another. Relationship and fellowship are not even reached through the same door. Relationship is through birth. Fellowship is possible only when each is pleasing to the other. An incident from our own family might throw further light on this.

One summer night just at dusk when John Mark was four years old he ran from his mother just as she stopped to push the wagon off the sidewalk. When she looked up he had vanished! Walking up and down the street she called loudly for him. No response. With our eleven-year-old daughter she hunted from the attic to the basement. By this time it was getting quite dark. In a frenzy of weeping my wife called the police. They were joined by about twenty college students who joined the search. After perhaps thirty minutes of anguish one of the students pulled back the heavy shrubs from the wall of a neighbor's house. There he stood hugging the wall. When he was asked why he didn't answer, he replied in a whisper, "I said, 'Here I am, Mother.' "

Mother's relief in finding her son did not deter her from administering a hard spanking. In a few minutes when daddy returned he received another—just to help him remember never to run away again. As you can imagine for a little while our fellowship was broken. The relationship of parent and child could never suffer in a momentary break.

Many children of God fail to live on that higher plane of fellowship with God. The apostle John knew what it meant to live in fellowship with God and he longed for every other Christian to experience it also. Under the guidance of the Holy Spirit he points out how this higher plane of Christian living can be attained. "Whoso keepeth his word, in him verily is the love of God perfected: hereby know we that we are in him" (2:5).

Let us not be confused over how sonship and fellowship are gained. Sonship is ours through the second birth and involves what Christ did. Fellowship is gained only when "we keep his Word."

John is especially concerned in this epistle about the Christian's fellowship with God and his Son, Jesus Christ. Fellowship, however, can only be enjoyed by those who like the same things. John records the things that Christ likes. First, he gives his own qualifications as an eyewitness for knowing the things that Christ liked. In 1:1–3 he states: "That which was from the beginning, which we have heard, which we have seen with our eyes, which we have looked upon, and our hands have handled, of the Word of life; (for the life was manifested, and we have seen it, and bear witness, and shew unto you that eternal life, which was with the Father, and was manifested unto us;) that which we have seen and heard declare we unto you, that ye also may have fellowship with us: and truly our fellowship is with the Father, and with his Son Jesus Christ."

Here is one John has *seen,* and *heard,* and *looked upon* and *touched.* He calls him the Word of life, the same name that was used in the Gospel, 1:14, where he definitely settles all questions as to who the Word is: "The Word was made flesh, and dwelt among us, (and we beheld his glory, the glory as of the only begotten of the Father)." Now, said John, I know him and have seen him, and have had fellowship with him. I write you what I know of him in order that you also may have fellowship with us, for our fellowship is actually with the Father and his Son.

I bring you fellowship.

Even as you have fellowship here with your earthly father I write you how you may have fellowship with your Heavenly Father. I know him and I know what he likes. Human experience demonstrates that friendships are made through knowing what another likes. To paraphrase John, "I know that person and I know what he likes, and I will tell you in order that you, too, may be his friend and have fellowship with him."

In 1 John 1:5 John repeats what he heard the Master say, "This then is the message which we have heard of him, and declare unto you, that God is light, and in him is no darkness at all." The apostle is reminding us that where God is there can be no darkness. In the beginning of creation God said, "Let there be light." John reiterates this truth that there can be no darkness in his presence.

Two facts John points out in verse 7, both actually happening when one walks in the light as he is in the light. We and God actually have fellowship, and since sin in no form can endure in his presence, cleansing for sin comes through the cross even as it did at salvation.

Lest we think that attainment of fellowship means the attainment of perfection, John writes that even those who walk in fellowship will be cleansed from all unrighteousness by his blood. If it were true that there were no sin in the life of one walking in fellowship with him, there would be no need of the cleansing by the blood. God does not cleanse that which needs no cleansing. This is in perfect accord with the next verse, "If we say that we have no sin, we deceive ourselves, and the truth is not in us." John is saying here that one who says he has no sin is lacking the truth. He does not yet grasp the great truth that even in fellowship with him the blood of Christ cleanses us from all sin.

Then in the following verse John says: "If we confess our sins, he is faithful and just to forgive us our sins, and to cleanse us from all unrighteousness." The word "confess" does not mean simply admitting verbally, but to make a heart acknowledgment of sin. This stand which a Christian takes constantly before God, that he is unworthy and in need of forgiveness, far outweighs a repetition to God, "I am a sinner." It was that cry which opened the gate of grace. A full realization of man's unworthiness and God's remedy will make us cry out unceasingly with Paul, "God forbid I should glory, save in the cross of our Lord Jesus Christ" (Gal. 6:14). As John urges men to climb to the highest level attainable for a Christian, he also writes indelibly upon the mind that even on that great plateau man must be constantly cleansed by the blood of Christ.

This knowledge of cleansing could well be part of the joy to which John refers when he states "that your joy may be full." Joy truly comes to him who finds that, though he has earnestly tried but not attained completely, God has promised, "If we walk in the light, as he is in the light, . . . the blood of Jesus Christ his Son, cleanseth us from all sin." Even when we fail, God looks at the attitude of the heart. "Man looketh on the outward appearance, but the Lord looketh on the heart" (1 Sam. 16:7).

John makes it very clear that if "we say we have fellowship with him, and walk in darkness, we lie." Many years ago as a college student I overheard a small group in the "dorm" talking about a girl whom I admired. Stopping a moment I heard one of the "playboys" remark that he had taken this girl out for a drink. They had parked, he said, and "she had gone the limit."

I could not believe what I heard, for I knew this girl well. The following day I met her roommate and asked her if Dorothy had gone out with Jim the night before.

"Why, no," said the girl, "she and Joyce and I stayed in our room all evening studying for a test. None of us even left the dormitory."

When I asked her if she were sure Dorothy had not had a date with Jim, she replied, "Dorothy said she would not be seen with him. Many times he has asked her for dates, but always she has refused."

It really wasn't necessary for me to learn that Jim had lied, for I knew this girl.

In a similar way the apostle John declares, in effect, "I know him. If a man says that he and God walk together in darkness he also lies, for when men walk in darkness they walk alone, not with God."

There are two groups to whom fellowship with God is impossible. First, the man who walks in darkness, and secondly, the man who will not keep his commandments. He that sayeth I know him and keepeth not his commandments is a liar (cf. 1 John 2:3). The first has reference to the man who insists on keeping his sin. The second is the man who will not do what God commands him to do. Perhaps there are more Christians out of fellowship with God, because they "refuse to do" than those who "refuse to give up their sin."

Recently I overheard a father repeatedly command his son to stop what he was doing. "Son," he said, "when I tell you to quit something I mean for you to quit. Nothing is as important for you to learn as that." A few minutes later I heard the father ask his little son to close the door which had blown open. Ignoring the request, the son continued with his play. This time his father went to him and said emphatically, "I told you a few minutes ago that nothing was as important for you to learn as obedience when I tell you to do something."

The boy looked up and said, "Daddy, that wasn't what you said. You said it was only important that I quit what you told me to quit." The father wisely admitted he had made a mistake. Then he tried to explain that it was not only important to quit when he was asked to but it was equally important to do what he was asked to do.

This is a truth that many Christians have not accepted.

They believe they can be pleasing to God if they only quit the things displeasing to him. They have not realized that when God gives a command it is equally as important to fulfil his command as it is to refrain from behavior displeasing to him.

The cost to a Christian who refuses to do God's will is his loss of God's unsearchable riches. Comparison of these treasures to the value of the sin for which he sacrificed these riches is small, indeed.

Standing on a street corner a missionary met an old friend. In their greetings to one another he pulled from his wallet the only picture he had left of his wife, who had died several years before. When their house burned, nothing was saved. After showing his wallet picture to his friend, he carelessly put it into his shirt pocket instead of his wallet and hurried across the street before a caravan of carts blocked the way. Just before he reached the other side of the unpaved street he looked down and saw an English penny, a coin worth two cents in American money. Stopping to pick it out of the mud, he discovered his wife's picture had fallen into the street. Quickly retracing his steps, he found the picture. The wheels of a cart had passed over it, mangling it in the gravel and dirt. Now the face of the picture could not even be recognized. Standing with the penny still in one hand and the marred picture in the other, tears filled his eyes. He lamented, "Yes, Penny, you are mine. I stooped to pick you up, but you cost me the most precious thing I had in this world!"

Many a Christian in eternity who has missed the riches which God intended for him, and remembering how little he received in return will also say, "Yes, I stopped to pick you up, but you cost me the most precious thing of all—my fellowship with God."

The message of 1 John is that there is a place of fellowship with God which the Christian may enter, but the place is attainable only to him who will say, "Thy will be done" —in both refraining from actions displeasing to God and in actively carrying out his commands.

5.

"Then Are Ye My Disciples Indeed"

"Then said Jesus to those Jews which believed on him, If ye continue in my word, then are ye my disciples indeed" (John 8:31).

In this Scripture our Lord was addressing those who already were believers. He was inviting them to come now and become disciples. You will note the distinction Jesus made between salvation and discipleship.

In order to better understand the meaning of discipleship we must become acquainted with the customs of that day. From place to place went many teachers who gathered about them men who were willing to learn. These were commonly known as disciples. To qualify as a follower one was required to leave home and friends and be willing to journey with his teacher. The term "discipleship" had no definite limit, for at one time our Lord may have had five thousand, but in John 6:66, we read that "from that time many of his disciples went back, and walked no more with him."

In Christ's day, "discipleship" denoted a follower, or learner. In our day we have no right to substitute a lesser meaning. We may note that the New Testament has many references to "John's disciples," which certainly did not mean they were saved through John, but were followers of John. Our Lord's one yearning was that those who believed on him as the Son of God would become his disciples, leaving all to follow him daily.

In Luke 14:25–26, Jesus pictured discipleship as a feast for those already saved. "A certain man made a great supper, and bade many: and sent his servant at supper time to say to them that were bidden, Come: for all things are now ready" (vv. 16–17). The supper is a picture of fellowship. It is an invitation for our time as well as theirs—fellowship with a living, glorified Redeemer! Surely no one would turn down such an unusual invitation, but we read: "They all with one consent began to make excuse. The first said unto him, I have bought a piece of ground, and I must needs go and see it: I pray thee have me excused. . . . And another said, I have married a wife, and therefore I cannot come" (vv. 18–20). They rejected his invitation, because they would not leave the things to which they were already attached.

In the parable of the sower we find the same reason given why God's Word does not prosper in the hearts of men. The cares of the world, the deceitfulness of riches, and the desire for other things have kept men busy, and have thwarted their spiritual growth. Blinded by earthly things they have missed the banquet of God.

"I say unto you, that none of those men which were bidden shall taste of my supper" (v. 24). Refusal to accept his invitation now meant rejection of his fellowship, loss of communion with him. "Go now and invite even those who are poor and maimed and halt [those with far less talent than those who had been invited]."

Then our Lord turned to the people standing there, including those who had believed on him, and said: "If any man come to me, and hate [that is, in the sense of indifference to or relative disregard for them in comparison with his attitude toward God (*Amplified New Testament:* Zondervan)] not his father, and mother, and wife, and children, and brethren, and sisters, yea, and his own life also, he cannot be my disciple" (v. 26). Although they had come to him for salvation, they were not willing to leave all and become disciples. Through the centuries his pleading voice is still reminding us that his requirements for discipleship are ever the same. "Whosoever doth not bear his cross, and come after me, cannot be my disciple" (v. 27). Discipleship is not a state one enters lightly or carelessly.

Knowing then that in a moment of enthusiasm some might decide too quickly to become his disciples Jesus said, "Which of you, intending to build a tower, sitteth not down first, and counteth the cost, whether he have sufficient to finish it? Lest haply, after he hath laid the foundation, and is not able to finish it, all that behold it begin to mock him, saying, This man began to build, and was not able to finish" (28–30). There is a danger of offering to become a disciple and then turning back, only to bring shame upon oneself and discredit to the Lord's name.

From a fair consideration of this parable one must definitely conclude that our Lord's invitation here is not to become a Christian, but to enter into discipleship. The invitation to accept salvation never includes a self appraisal to determine one's power to hold out. If so, no man could accept. The invitation to become a child of God has two requirements only—faith in Christ and submission to his will.

Discipleship is an even closer relationship to Christ. For this involvement a man must search his soul, count the cost, and determine whether he is willing to put Christ first in all areas of his life. Thus the Lord said, "So likewise, whosoever he be of you that forsaketh not all that he hath, he cannot be my disciple" (v. 33). Jesus meant his words to be severe. He wanted his hearers to count the cost.

On the east coast of Newfoundland a storm arose, and not a ship was able to reach shore. All night long wives, mothers, children, sweethearts paced up and down the beach, waiting and praying for their loved ones. Toward morning, to add to the horror, a cottage caught fire. Without the men, the women were unable to put out the blaze.

By dawn the storm had ceased. Streaks of sunrise lighted the horizon, and the entire fishing fleet was safe in the harbor. Everyone rejoiced, but one mother. Tearfully she told her husband their home had burned.

Embracing her, the husband cried, "Thank God for the fire! It was by the light of our burning cottage that the whole fleet found its way into port."

The fires of sacrifice for Christ always brings gladness and peace and self-fulfilment. Do we have the courage to honestly ask, "Have we forsaken all?" If we cannot answer in the affirmative we have no right to claim discipleship. "Whosoever he be of you that forsaketh not all that he hath, he cannot be my disciple" (v. 33).

In contrast the Lord showed the other side of the coin when he alluded to the tragedy of a life without dedication to him. He used as a frame of reference the common season-ing—salt. "Salt is good: but if the salt have lost its savour, wherewith shall it be seasoned?" (vv. 34–35). God needs salty Christians to bring flavor and preservation to his world. To have no "taste" is to have no power.

For this reason later Paul wrote: "I beseech you there-fore, brethren, by the mercies of God, that ye present your bodies a living sacrifice, holy, acceptable unto God, which is your reasonable service . . . that ye may prove what is that good, and acceptable, and perfect, will of God" (Rom. 12:1–2). It is only as we yield our lives to him that we become a blessing. The cost may be great, but the glory far excels the sacrifice.

In the vault in London there is a replica of the great Culinan diamond, weighing over a pound. One day it seemed the master jeweler was destroying this precious jewel, for he broke it into nine smaller sets. But after the cutting there came a new glory, the greatest probably ever given to any jewel, for now they grace the crown of Queen Elizabeth.

The Master's day was little different from our own. When the journey became difficult many turned back. Even Peter for a time gave up his discipleship when he denied the Lord. When the news reached him that the Lord had arisen he must have doubted that Christ would ever include him again in the inner circle. But Jesus, knowing Peter's sorrow and anguish, sent him a special message to follow him into Galilee. To the women the angel at the empty tomb said, "Go your way, tell his disciples *and Peter*" (Mark 16:7).

It is easy to imagine the utter gladness of Peter when he received that message of forgiveness. Jesus was giving him another opportunity for service. Such love through the ages has again and again called believers back from their weaknesses and failures to take up the cross of discipleship and follow him. Discipleship becomes a reality only when the Christian's actual surrender measures up to his teaching. One cannot sing "Have Thine own way, Lord! . . . Mold me and make me after Thy will" and then say, "Pray have me excused." If one is to become a disciple then "Thy kingdom come; thy will be done" cannot be followed by even the weakest no. If one is to become a disciple then "Seek ye first the kingdom of God, and his righteousness" means the priority of God's claim over one's own desires.

In summary we may conclude that the land of discipleship, fellowship, sanctification, and the Spirit-filled life will be reached by the Christian who accepts the second cross. But many believers will shrink from this self-surrender, and will walk no more with him in discipleship, for they have found the saying too hard to accept. For them the first cross is a reality; the second cross is an untested theory. They are not willing to let go of self.

Desperately a boy clung to a shrub growing out of the steep cliffs on an England coast. Falling from the top he had grabbed the bush. No one seemed to hear his shouts. Darkness was falling. Then above him a light appeared and a man's voice cried, "Let go!" Was the man foolish? Did he want him harmed? Again came the words, "Let go!" His arms were aching. He could struggle no more. He obeyed, and slipped four feet to solid ground! Only his struggles had kept him from security.

6.
"Thou Shalt Be a Blessing"

The cost of being out of fellowship with God is revealed in the Old Testament as well as in the New. God's plan for the early believers was for them to live in the Land of Promise and to become a blessing to all mankind.

Several facts are highlighted in the story of Abraham and Lot that reveal how closely God's will for the patriarchs resembles his plan for Christians today. First, there is a place in which God intended each should live. In the Old Testament it is called the Land of Promise. In the New Testament it is called the place of fellowship. Only in this place is God's special love, protection, and blessings known.

Lot selfishly chose what he believed to be the most fertile, and thus the most economically profitable section of the land. Ignoring the right of his Uncle Abraham, patriarch and leader, he thought only of his own gain. Apparently at this epoch in his life he had forgotten that he had joined Abraham in his call to follow God to a new Land of Promise. The wealth and power of the Dead Sea cities of Sodom and Gomorrah temporarily erased his vision of what God had planned for him. His selfish decision could have but one ending, for one day, rescued by two angels, he fled with his family from the destruction of the cities, leaving all his investments to turn to ashes.

But Lot suffered even more. Disregarding the angel's command not to look back, Lot's wife turned into a pillar of salt, a temptation to which she would not have been exposed had Lot not separated himself from fellowship with God's people. His daughters, feeling the need of children, made their father drunk and conceived by him. The descendants of these sons became the Moabites and Ammonites, later to become thorns in the side of Israel. What a daily regret he must have felt as he paid the cost of his selfish decision!

Years later Jacob also fled from the Land of Promise to live in the land of his Uncle Laban. Through his desire to acquire the birthright which encompassed not only receiving the leadership of the family but also a double share of the inheritance he and his mother, Rebecca, outwitted and deceived Isaac into giving the younger son the blessing.

If we take into account Rebecca's desire to carry out the will of the Lord, we can understand her motivation in wanting the twin son, Jacob, to get the birthright. "The Lord said unto her, Two nations are in thy womb, and two manner of people shall be separated from thy bowels; and the one people shall be stronger than the other people; and the elder shall serve the younger" (Gen. 25:23).

We cannot know whether Rebecca recognized the timeless law of God that wrong methods never bring right ends. Clutching her favorite son to her in a farewell embrace, she said, "Flee thou to Laban my brother to Haran; and tarry with him a few days, until thy brother's fury turn away;

until thy brother's anger turn away from thee, and he forget
that which thou hast done to him; then I will send, and fetch
thee from thence" (27:43–45). That day she could not
know that her deception would rob her of ever seeing her
son again.

And what of Jacob? He recognized the deception to be
wrong. He "said to Rebekah his mother, Behold, Esau my
brother is a hairy man, and I am a smooth man: my father
per adventure will feel me, and I shall seem to him as a
deceiver; and I shall bring a curse upon me, and not a
blessing. And his mother said unto him, Upon me be thy
curse, my son: only obey my voice" (27:11–13).

This gives us an explanation of the marvelous vision that
came to the lonely young Jacob as he fled from a brother
who threatened to kill him. Pillowing his head on a stone he
dreamed of a celestial ladder stretching from earth to
heaven with angels ascending and descending and the Lord
at the very top. In this holy place he heard the voice of God
say, "I am the Lord God of Abraham thy father, and the
God of Isaac: the land whereon thou liest, to thee will give
it, and to thy seed; and thy seed shall be as the dust of the
earth . . . and in thee and in thy seed shall all the families
of the earth be blessed. And, behold, I am with thee, and
will keep thee in all places whither thou goest, and will
bring thee again into this land" (28:13–15).

"Jacob awaked out of his sleep, and he said, Surely the
Lord is in this place; and I knew it not . . . this is none
other but the house of God, and this is the gate of heaven
(vv. 16–17).

Although Jacob had experienced the wondrous presence
of God and had heard his voice of promise, he was destined

to suffer for his deception. The law of sowing and reaping is immutable. In the years that followed in the house of Laban he suffered first the deception of receiving Leah, instead of his beloved Rachel, at the wedding bed. Fourteen years, instead of seven, he had to work to pay for Rachel, and his wages were changed ten times.

When twenty years had gone by and dissension had arisen between Jacob and the sons of Laban, "the Lord said unto Jacob, Return unto the land of thy fathers, and to thy kindred; and I will be with thee" (31:3)

Coupled with Jacob's desire to follow the command of God was also his deep yearning to be reconciled with his brother Esau. Before reentering the Promised Land Jacob had to undergo a struggle which permanently changed him, both physically and spiritually. Coming to the Jabbok River he sent ahead servants with presents of flocks and herds to be delivered to his brother.

Then alone on the banks of the river, Jacob wrestled with a man until the dawn. "When he saw that he prevailed not against him, he touched the hollow of his thigh; and the hollow of Jacob's thigh was out of joint, as he wrestled with him. And he said, Let me go, for the day breaketh. And he said, I will not let thee go, except thou bless me. And he said unto him, What is thy name? And he said, Jacob. [meaning 'he takes by the heel' or 'supplanter']. And he said, Thy name shall be called no more Jacob, but Israel: for as a prince hast thou power with God and with men, and hast prevailed. . . . And so Jacob called the name of the place Peniel: for I have seen God face to face, and my life is preserved" (32:25–31).

In patriarchal days it was believed that a person's self

was concentrated in his name. Thus, the giving to Jacob of a new name by God signified a *new self*. Instead of supplanter, or trickster, he received the new name Israel, meaning "God rules." This was an affirmation of his total commitment to God and his plan for his life. This also was the beginning of Jacob's life in becoming a blessing.

This climactic encounter with God not only changed his name and his life but also prepared Jacob for the dreaded experience of seeing his brother's face. For twenty years he had lived for this hour. Would hate and murder still be in his brother's heart? How many times he must have ached for his forgiveness!

The glory of that meeting of estranged brothers is recorded thus: when Jacob meets Esau he exclaims "I have seen thy face, as though I had seen the face of God" (33:10). The new person, Israel (God rules), looked into the rough, rugged, bearded face of his brother and saw God! This is the glory of human experience touched by the power of God—to see God's face in our fellowman. Reconciliation, peace, and joy came to Jacob when he obeyed God in returning to the land God planned for him and to reconciliation with his brother. This new self was full of love for his brother. Essentially this act can be identified with the command of our Lord in the New Testament when he commanded those who would follow him "to take up the cross and follow me."

7.
Are You "There"?

God has not only promised care and protection to the Christian in accord with his will, he has also promised blessings beyond belief. There are some promises that can be claimed only by the man in accord with God's purpose. Here are just a few of them.

"Seek ye first the kingdom of God and his righteousness; and all these things shall be added unto you" (Matt. 6:33).

"Whose keepeth his word, in him verily is the love of God perfected: hereby know we that we are in him" (1 John 2:5).

"All things work together for good to them that love God, to them who are the called according to his purpose" (Rom. 8:28).

Through the years I have seen many young married couples enter college with very little money, but with a big dream. They envision the day when they will reach an economic level which will enable their children to attend college, a level which will rid them of economic fears. In order to reach this goal they begin four long years of hard work and self-denial. In their most difficult hours some of them have come to my office with almost unsolvable problems. One of these at commencement time said to me jubilantly, "Well, we made it!" Then he stepped out of the graduation line to say, "You know, I wouldn't be in this procession if you hadn't counseled me as you did that day. I was discouraged and ready to quit. But you said, 'Many students fighting their way up find rough going, but some of you are going to move up to a higher level where it is easier. No one can prevent your being one of that group, and no one can keep you from remaining where you are now.' "

During my years as a pastor I gave the same advice to many Christians who were floundering and faltering on a low spiritual level. No man can keep you from staying where you are, but God himself has declared there is a plateau higher up where all things work together for good.

The great truth concerning special protection and care for the man in God's will does not appear for the first time in the New Testament. The Old Testament Scriptures abound in contrasts between the man who is *in* God's purpose and the man who is *out* of God's will.

Psalm 91 was written as a promise to the man who is in the right place, the place in accord with God's will. "He that dwelleth in the secret place of the most High shall abide under the shadow of the Almighty. . . . He shall cover thee with his feathers. . . . A thousand shall fall at thy side, and ten thousand at thy right hand, but it shall not come nigh thee" (vv. 1–7). These blessings are conditioned, however: He that dwelleth in the secret place of the most High; he who has made the Lord his dwelling place; he who has set his love and affection upon the Lord. In other words, to the person in fellowship with God is the promise given.

The first Psalm also is a contrast between two men, one choosing his own way and the other considering God's will both day and night. "Blessed is the man that walketh not in the counsel of the ungodly, nor standeth in the way of sinners, nor sitteth in the seat of the scornful. But his delight is in the law of the Lord; and in his law doth he meditate day and night. And he shall be like a tree planted by the rivers of water, that bringeth forth his fruit in his season; his leaf also shall not wither; and whatsoever he doeth shall prosper." His delight is in the Lord! No wonder God compares him to a tree whose roots reach forth into the very rivers of water, and therefore whatsoever he does shall prosper.

To the man who gives all to God there come these promises to him: (1) All things will be added to him who seeks first his kingdom; (2) all things work together for good for those in accord with his will.

Elijah needed bread and found it waiting when he came to God's appointed place. Samson needed strength, and God gave it when his will was done. Peter needed courage and found it when the Holy Spirit filled him. Paul needed relief from the thorn in the flesh and found it in complete abandonment of the flesh. The Syro-Phoenician woman crying for help for her daughter found it when she sought help for herself first. Her cry that went unanswered was "Help my daughter!" When she saw her own need first and cried, "Help me!" then Jesus said, "O woman, great is thy faith: be it unto thee even as thou wilt. And her daughter was made whole from that very hour" (Matt. 15:28).

One cannot help but notice the parallel between Elijah's experience and the experience promised one who practices the principles laid down in the Lord's prayer. When Elijah said, "Thy will be done," and gave up the false security of the juniper tree to go to the place God appointed to him he found the bread delivered by the ravens. When the Christian can say, as did Elijah, "Thy will be done," he, too, can immediately claim the right to pray, "Give us this day our daily bread." In earlier days the Israelites also found their bread (manna) delivered daily when God's plan was followed to the letter. Through all ages it is quite evident that God's will is to provide daily bread to the one who is in accord with his purpose.

But one can as surely lose these blessings by being in the *wrong* place as he can claim them by being in the *right* place. A good example of this truth is the experience of Thomas. When he failed to be in the appointed place when the others saw the risen Lord, he doubted. For a whole week he could have had their gladness instead of his misery and skepticism. And what about Peter? Had he been close to the Lord instead of the enemy he would not have denied the Master. In contrast to these, however, Philip was in accord with God's purpose for him. When the voice of the Holy Spirit called him from the revival in Samaria to go to Gaza, he was ready for God's appointment for him with the Ethiopian eunuch, treasurer of the country of Ethiopia. These are only a few examples illustrating the truth that God provides and guides his children who are in accord with his will.

The big mistake some Christians make is in trying to claim promises without meeting the conditions. It is presumptuousness personified for Christians who are living in the desert to attempt to claim the blessings which God has promised only to those who reach the Promised Land, to which God would bring every man. These Christians are like children to whom a father has made a conditional promise. They forget the conditions and insistently plead, "You promised! you promised!" Like these children, some Christians come to the Lord saying, "Lord, you promised," but God promised only to give his blessings to those who obeyed his commands. God must be saddened, even as is a father, because we listen so poorly, interpret so wildly, and claim so brazenly.

One cannot keep from comparing the destitute, despairing, and discouraged Elijah under the juniper tree saying no to God with the victorious Elijah being fed by the ravens at the Brook Cherith after saying an unqualified yes to God. One has only to see the haste with which Elijah reached the place God had appointed for him. Few have equaled his record in reaching the God-appointed place. He covered some seventy miles without stopping, a record speed for his day.

From the pages of missionary history there are many illustrations of the provisions and protections of God. In the early days of America David Brainerd felt called of God to take the gospel to the Indians. He could not turn away from the challenge of taking the good news to the fiercest tribe of all—Indians who had become embittered against the white man. The greed and firewater of the white man had hindered the progress of genuine Christianity among the original inhabitants of our great continent.

This savage tribe lived in a retreat from which they stealthily raided the white settlers. To win these savage Indians to Christ so aroused Brainerd's ardor that he resolved to go among them alone and unarmed, although at this time he was in poor health. He carried with him a little tent. At length he reached the vicinity of the principal village of the tribe. He pitched his little white tent, and then resolved to spend some time in prayer before he began his witness.

While he was alone with God in his tent the sharp eyes of some Indian hunters had been watching him while he pitched his tent, and then had hurried away to inform the chief.

A hasty council was held. How could a white man dare pitch his tent without their consent! Their unanimous verdict was death. A group of warriors were sent off with orders to kill instantly, and scalp the white man for invading their hunting grounds. When they reached the neighborhood of Mr. Brainerd's tent they hid in sheltered places and waited for the missionary to come out. Then they would shoot him with their arrows. But while they waited the man of God was on his knees in prayer, pleading for the companionship and help of him who had promised, "My presence shall go with thee."

With little patience to wait the Indians decided that only three or four of them would get close enough to see what he was doing. There they saw the missionary on his knees with his back toward them, utterly unconscious of their presence. To them he seemed in earnest conversation with another, whom they could not see, but who must surely be visible to him, or he would not continue to talk so earnestly to him.

As they gazed their superstitious nature was awed and subdued, and they felt they dared not injure the man. But they continued to watch, as though riveted to the ground.

Just then a great rattle snake pushed its ugly head under the side curtains of the tent and glided in, crawling straight to the feet of Brainerd—even crawling over them. Yet it did not strike, but glided under the tent disappearing in the tall grass.

The startled Indians noiselessly drew back and joined their comrades in the forest, describing to them what they had seen. The missionary had been so engrossed in prayer he knew nothing of the visit of the snake or of the savages. Arising from his knees, he knew nothing of how the Indians would react to him.

To his great astonishment and delight, it seemed as if the whole village welcomed him as an old friend. Gladly they listened to his teaching, and in time many of them were converted. Through him God wrought a marvelous transformation in this fierce tribe.

The key to God's blessing both for Elijah and for the Christian today is to be "there," in the place God wills. There is a place where God has appointed for every man to be, even as there was a place that God appointed for Elijah.

8.
"That Ye May Know"

"That which we have seen and heard declare we unto you, that ye also may have fellowship with us: and truly our fellowship is with the Father, and with his Son Jesus Christ" (1 John 1:3).

The two great doctrines of salvation and assurance are the themes of John's writing. In his Gospel, John writes, "These are written, that ye might believe that Jesus is the Christ, the Son of God; and that believing ye might have life through his name" (20:31). In his First Epistle he writes, "These things have I written to you that [already] believe . . . *that ye may know that ye have eternal life*" (5:13). The Gospel and the Epistle are supplementary. In the Gospel is found *the way* to eternal life. In the Epistle is found the way *to know that one has eternal life*.

John's Gospel points the way to salvation—through faith in Jesus Christ as Saviour. He even concluded by saying that his purpose in writing was that readers and hearers would believe in the Son of God. In John's First Epistle his purpose is to show that fellowship with Christ is dependent upon the believer's life and works. In summary it may be concluded that sonship is by the second birth and fellowship with God is by works, faith in action—bearing the second cross.

The three inseparables in this gospel are believing in Christ, sonship now, eternal life hereafter. The three inseparables in this epistle are not belief in him, but rather keeping his commandments; not the gaining of eternal life, but the joy of knowing that we do possess eternal life now. The truth we find here may be put in this simple outline:

(1) That you may have *fellowship*
(2) That *you may know you have eternal life*
(3) That *your joy may be full"*

John thus makes clear that not only is there a place of fellowship with God but also it is only in that land where certain precious fruit can be had.

Some years ago on a preaching mission to Florida I was enjoying the warmth of the sun and searching my mind for an appropriate illustration for fellowship with God. Just then I heard the radio announcer give the weather report in Kentucky. As he was saying "below zero" I reached up and picked an orange off the tree. Suddenly I realized I had my illustration. I had come out of one part of the country into another and was enjoying the blessings made possible only to those living in that place. John declares there is a place to which God would lead the Christian where the fruits are many.

Two of these fruits he emphasizes. The first is *joy*. The second he stresses is *knowledge that we are God's children*. But both of these fruits are conditional upon our keeping his commandments.

The fact of sin and God's cleansing of our sin John deals

with in 1 John 1:7 to 2:2. In 2:3 he again returns to the
purpose for which he wrote the book—that we may know
that we are saved. "Hereby we know that we know him, if
we keep his commandments." He does not say "hereby do
we know him," but rather "hereby do we *know* we know
him." Our assurance of salvation is dependent upon our
keeping his commandments and doing the things pleasing in
his sight. Some have erroneously concluded that John
teaches here that by keeping his commandments we become
the children of God. This is not the case, for John is writing
to those who have already become Christians, urging them
to keep his commandments in order that they might also
have *fellowship* with him. Sonship is theirs already; fellowship, joy, assurance can be achieved only through keeping
his commandments.

John mentions no specific sin that hinders fellowship
until verse 9. Although we know there are many sins which
prevent fellowship with God, John singles out this one
especially as the cardinal sin preventing fellowship. "He
that saith he is in the light, and hateth his brother, is in
darkness even until now." May I paraphrase it thus: He that
saith he is in the light [fellowship] with God and hates his
brother has not come into that fellowship. But he that
loveth his brother abideth in the light [where God is] and
there is no reason for him to stumble. He has removed the
stumbling stone to fellowship by loving his brother.

Again in 1 John 3:10 John warns Christians that lack
of love for a brother destroys fellowship with God. The
disciple is echoing the very words of the Master, "Thou
shalt love the Lord thy God with all thy heart . . . and thy
neighbor as thyself. This is the first and great command-

ment" (Matt. 22:37–39). When a man's life is motivated and controlled by love, his acts will be right, as surely as the ship's journey will be right when the needle on the compass is fixed on the North Star. It is only when the needle is not fixed and sure and the ship is off course that the navigator must search for each individual rock and danger. These appear only in the path of a ship or a man who is off course. What is this course God has mapped out for the Christian? *It is that he love the Lord with all his heart and his neighbor as himself*. To this the Christian compass must forever point. Only then will the journey be completed and the law and prophets fulfilled.

Now comes the conclusion in 1 John 3:18–19: "My little children, let us not love in word, neither in tongue; but in deed and in truth. And hereby we know that we are of the truth, and shall assure our hearts before him." Thus, our knowledge and the assurance of our hearts comes because of our fellowship and this is possible only when we have love for our brothers. Moreover, in verse 21 John states that it is through this love for our brothers that we have confidence toward God and are assured that all things are right between us and our Lord.

All Scriptures bear out the theme and purpose of John's writing: "Thou shalt love the Lord thy God"—theme of the Gospel, "Thou shalt love thy neighbor as thyself"—theme of the Epistle. Through Christ's love for us we obtain sonship with God. Through our love for Christ we have fellowship and assurance of our salvation. How wretched to be out of fellowship with God and lack the assurance which could be ours! This is not what God intended for his children. He wants us to enjoy fellowship with him, to have assurance of eternal life, and to experience joy to the fullest.

Many defeated, unhappy Christians resemble the man who was crossing the ocean to America on one of the luxury liners. Day after day he stood outside the dining salon, smelling the good food and yearning for a meal, yet resigning himself to crackers and cheese which he munched in his stateroom. Finally, on the last day out, smelling the good food, he stopped the steward and asked, "What would it cost me to have just one meal in there?"

The steward replied, "Let me see your ticket." Looking at it the astonished steward exclaimed, "Why, man, it will cost you nothing! Your ticket calls for three meals a day in the dining salon. You were entitled to them all the way across."

Many Christians have missed God's banquet in life, not realizing that it would be theirs "if they kept his commandments and did the things pleasing in his sight."

How superbly is this expressed in 1 John 2:5: "But whoso keepeth his word, in him verily is the love of God perfected; hereby know we that we are in him." By keeping his commandments and pleasing him we experience God's love brought into full bloom, for that is the root meaning of "perfect." The thought of "full expression" is also found in the meaning of this word. Thus, God is able to fully express himself to the child who is obedient and in fellowship with him. Only as we are in accord with his will can he do that for us which his love embodies—that of giving us the joy of knowing we possess eternal life.

When our first daughter was two years old she was sick for several days. Every night during the illness her mother went to her room and stayed with her until she went to sleep. Even after she became well she continued to expect mother to stay with her until dreams carried her away. When this had to be discontinued and mother left the room, she disobeyed by coming down the stairs. We ushered her back upstairs. She continued to come down the stairs. Finally, as a last resort we fastened her door. Then she cried as if her heart would break. She was sure we did not love her. But her disobedience kept us from expressing our love. We longed to take her into our arms that she might know our love was sure, but we could not because of her disobedience.

That is a picture of what John is saying in his First Epistle. If we keep his word then God can express his love (brought into full bloom) and then our joy will be full in knowing that we are his. The fruit of knowing can only be found at a higher level and can only be claimed by the one who attains and keeps this level on which fellowship alone is possible.

9.
The Answer in the Sanctuary

For those who hesitate to pick up the second cross there is a ring of familiarity in the questions asked by the psalmist. What he observed around him caused him to doubt his convictions. When he saw the wicked prosper and the righteous being punished it almost knocked him off his feet. "My steps had well nigh slipped." He did not understand until he reached a higher level of Christian experience. The key to understanding this apparent injustice which God permits, as well as the great riches available to the Christian is reserved only for those in fellowship with God (the secret place). But when he enters this place, through the door of self-denial, *then* he understands (v. 1). *Then* "all things work together for good" (Rom. 8:28); "ask what ye will, and it shall be done unto you" (John 15:7), "he shall be a vessel . . . sanctified and meet for the Master's use" (2 Tim. 2:21); "all these things shall be added" (Matt. 6:33).

It is not surprising to find many a Christian like the psalmist, knocked off his feet when he saw the prosperity of the wicked (v. 2), but when "I went into the sanctuary of

God; then understood I their end" (Psalm 73:17). Is there a Christian who at some time has not asked, "Does it really pay to be a Christian?" From the physical plane alone man could well conclude that the wicked have chosen the better way.

One day while passing the most elegant and expensive home in the community where I pastored I saw a boy riding his bicycle in the yard. Pausing for a moment I asked him where his family attended church. His answer indicated they used to attend the church I was serving. As I looked along the back wall of the large three-car garage I could readily understand why the church and God had no place in their lives. Lined up the entire length of the garage was a row of gambling machines. My face clouded as I looked at this youth and others like him who would be injured by them, because of one man's greed for personal gain. For a moment the question popped into my own mind, "Does it pay to be a Christian, after all?" Any man who asks this question will find his answer if he studies the four scenes of Psalm 73.

In scene 1 the writer stands looking about him at the prosperity of the wicked (vv. 4–11).

In scene 2 he compares the prosperity of the wicked with his own prosperity (vv. 12–16).

In scene 3 the man stands with God as God reveals the future to him (vv. 17–19).

In scene 4 the man looks for the second time at the wicked, but now the things of the world have grown strangely dim (vv. 20–28).

In scene 1 the benefits all seem to be in favor of the man who leaves God out of his life.

In verse 4 there is indication of no difference in the death experience itself for the saved and the lost. "There are no bands in their death."

In verse 5 he does not even have as much trouble in life as the Christian. "They are not in trouble as other men."

In verse 6 they are proud and violent—and get by with it. They are proud. Violence covers them as a garment. If there is one word which characterizes a man who leaves God out of his life, it is that he is violent, or self-willed. The one central fact of his life is ignoring man's law and God's law. In fact, he ignores all law and is dominated only by self-will.

Some years ago in a pastorate I met such a man. He was arrogant, self-sufficient, proud, self-willed, and prosperous. As I spoke to him of the Saviour he scoffed at the idea of God and future justice. Nothing seemed sacred to him. His whole attitude was, "Where is the God you're talking about? Why, even if there were a God, he doesn't know I am here."

Before I left him I replied, "Friend, God not only knows you are here but he has even described you in Psalm 73." I read the psalm, and as he listened, the man turned to me in deep concern, for at least one time in his life that described his life and attitude.

In verse 10 we find the reason why this believer was almost knocked off his feet. He was struck at a most vital point—through his family. The psalmist declares, "Waters of a full cup are wrung out to" his people. His family has plenty because of his prosperity. At this point a man is most vulnerable and often misled.

The scene changes in verses 12–15. The man who has

been looking at the prosperity of the wicked now begins to compare his own situation with that of the unbeliever. His comparison begins with the meaningful word, "Behold!"—stop! look! listen! It is time he stops to consider and evaluate the situation. His conclusion is that the ungodly have ignored thy ways and they prosper in the world. I have cleansed my heart and purified my hands in vain, for I have been punished instead of receiving prosperity. My efforts to live a godly life have been futile. I have not received fair treatment, and yet I have to keep quiet about it. If I should speak out I would offend the other believers (cf. v. 15). Not only am I punished unjustly—but I do not dare speak of it. The treatment I have received is even too painful for me to think about (cf. v. 16).

The psalmist had reached an all-time low in his spiritual experience, but in this hour of utter dejection and despair he discovered the answer and has passed it on to every believer of every age. "It was too painful for me; *until* I went into the sanctuary of God" (vv. 16–17). Then God pulled back the curtain and the writer looked into the future (v. 17). The scene has changed for the second time, for the writer stands now with God as he reveals to him the end awaiting the godless man who apparently prospers so well now. We hear the writer cry out: All I could see was what was happening about me, until God opened my eyes and showed me that end which awaited the arrogant man. "Surely thou didst set them in slippery places: thou castedst them down into destruction. How are they brought into desolation, as in a moment! They are utterly consumed with terrors" (vv. 18–19).

While a student at college I was driving with my family

from Louisville. During the night a snow had fallen, followed by rain that froze as it fell. Both the papers and radio warned of hazardous roads. In addition to these warnings I had the continual sharp warnings of Mother and Dad who sat with me in the front seat. Every time I increased the speed a little, I received a gentle but determined nudge from Mother. That was eloquent enough for me to slow down.

The situation as I saw it was made even worse when another car sounded the horn and whizzed by us——and he didn't slip! In my boyish thinking I resented his going fast if I could not. I confess, I hoped he would slip! As I saw him go over the hill and out of sight I said to myself, "Now he is right. Here we are poking along, when we might be covering the miles as fast as he. Rebelling inwardly and fuming over the enforced controls put on my driving, I self-pityingly continued our journey.

Several miles ahead I slowed up for a line of cars that had stopped to help a driver who had slipped off the road. Getting out of the car to investigate I noticed his leg was broken, his wife's face severely cut. They were being helped into another car to be rushed to the hospital. The car that had wrecked looked vaguely familiar. Suddenly I discovered it was the car that had passed me. Then I recalled my thoughts as he passed me. "We ought to be going like that." But seeing the end of the incident I concluded with the psalmist, "Surely thou didst set them in slippery places: thou castedst them down into destruction."

During my boyhood I walked with my family to church, a mile from our home. Dad held my hand and Mother held my sister's. To me it was absurd and degrading for him to hold my hand——especially when we were joined by a neighboring family with several children. Since the parents could not hold the hands of all, they held only the hand of the youngest. They never held the hand of the boy my age. To irritate me even more he would stick out his tongue as he ran by me, and whisper, "Sissy!" (He usually paid for that the next day on our way to school.)

One night I tried my old trick of waiting until Dad became engaged in an interesting conversation with the neighbor on politics and slipped my hand from his. But I pulled too soon and Dad tightened his grip. Just about that time my tormentor passed by with the usual routine whispering of "Sissy." As I planned what I would do to him the next day I suddenly heard a splash! It was a cold November day, and it wasn't hard to guess someone had fallen in one of the many mud puddles on that road. The men hurried over with the lantern—and there was my tormentor with mud all over him, cold, wet, and shivering. I admit shamefacedly I was glad. But I learned something that night which has come to me often through the years. *The same hand which held me back, also held me up,* for there I stood warm, happy, and dry. The Christian, too, is not permitted to go everywhere others go because of God's restraining hand. But he can say with the psalmist, "Thou hast holden me by my right hand."

10.
Rewards

"If any man's work abide which he hath built thereupon, he shall receive a reward" (1 Cor. 3:14).

The two stages of man's Christian experience are compared to the two phases of constructing a building: laying the foundation and the erection of the building. Special attention should be given to the fact that when man appears on the project the foundation has already been laid, "for other foundation can no man lay than that is laid, which is Jesus Christ" (1 Cor. 3:11). Of equal importance is the fact that the building on the foundation must be put up by man. Here again are pictured the two parts of the Christian experience. First, that which Christ has done for man—the foundation which no man can lay. And next, the part which man does for himself—the construction of a building upon this foundation. The type of construction is solely up to the man. One of God's greatest challenges to man is given here. A man may build a house comparable to gold, silver, or even precious stones. Or he may erect what God describes as a thatched hut made of grass or stubble.

Too much emphasis cannot be placed on the great care

and concern man should use in his building, because it will
be appraised by God himself. "Every man's work shall be
made manifest: for the day shall declare it, because it shall
be revealed by fire; and the fire shall try every man's work
of what sort it is" (v. 13). "If any man's work abide which
he hath built thereupon, he shall receive a reward" (v. 14).

It is the reality of rewards with which we deal in this
chapter. If one is to understand rewards he must first accept
the fact that a Christian's inheritance and his rewards are
different in every respect. We note again that the Christian
bearing the second cross will be in line for rewards.

We are born to an inheritance (Eph. 1:1). We work for
rewards. Our inheritance is already reserved (v. 14). Many
rewards are yet to be earned. Our inheritance is given to us
by Christ (v. 3). Our rewards depend on our actions and
attitudes. The inheritance for each Christian is the same (v.
14), but Christians will be given different rewards.

Several facts must be recognized, if one is to understand
rewards. It must be kept in mind that rewards are given for
deeds done after one experiences salvation. Our Lord compared the work done by two men to two houses that were
built. One man built on the rock; the other built on the
sand. It is stated that one house stood the storm, while the
other house fell because of the difference in the foundations.
The house that fell did so not because of inferior material or
workmanship, but because it rested on an unsound foundation. The truth emphasized in the parable is that identical
buildings may be erected by two men and one will stand the
storm and the other will fall. Man's work will not stand the
testing unless it is like the house built on a foundation
which is already laid before he starts to build. He simply

accepts the foundation as a gift, "for other foundation can no man lay than that is laid, which is Jesus Christ" (1 Cor. 3:11). The building (works of man) will not stand the testing unless he himself has first accepted Christ.

On the basis of reason alone man can accept this truth. Every day a man lives refusing Christ and thus rejecting him as Lord is a day lived in constant testimony against him. "For he that is not for me is against me." That man lives that day saying to all men, "As far as I am concerned he is not Lord. God claims that every knee should bow and every tongue should confess that he is Lord, but this *I* will not do." No good that man could do that day would offset the harm of rejecting Christ as Lord. No man can count on his works to save him without Christ, for until man accepts Christ his works will not even stand to be counted for him. Each day he comes up in the red.

Another truth concerning rewards is that they are given, not for everything good that man does, but for the good things that are done *in his name*. Some have incorrectly quoted, "He that giveth so much as a cup of cold water shall in no wise lose his reward." This is incorrect, for it omits the important words "in his name." When a Christian fails to connect his gift or deed with the cause of Christ, then he has failed in witnessing to the cause of Christ. For example, if a Christian gives food to another in need and does it only in his own name, those who know of the gift will honor the giver instead of the Christ who taught that it is more blessed to give than to receive. The Christian, rather than Christ, will receive the honor. When a Christian receives the honor here on earth he has received his reward. "Take heed that ye do not your alms before men, *to be seen of them:* other-

wise, ye have no reward of your Father which is in heaven"
(Matt. 6:1). If the deed is done through his church or if it
is acknowledged that the deed is done in obedience to our
Lord's command and because of love for him, then that
work qualifies for a reward.

Years ago while I was alone at the parsonage there came
a knock at the back door. Standing there was a man shab-
bily dressed. "I'm hungry," he said. This was one of the
depression years of breadlines when available jobs were
few. Inviting him in I heard his story of trying to find work
in Detroit. Having failed, he was hitchhiking back to Georgia. As he talked I was preparing a sandwich. As I did I was
thinking of Jesus' words, "I was hungry and ye fed me."

"I'm glad you came tonight," I said, "for you have given
me an opportunity to keep one of the commandments of my
Saviour, who told us to help one another. Tomorrow perhaps someone will need to help me." He stopped eating and
looked at me without a word. Soon he left and was on the
road again.

About a year later a big new car stopped in front of the
parsonage. It also was another late Sunday, and I was
putting the finishing touches on my evening message. Opening the door to the stranger I heard him ask, "You don't
remember me, do you?"

Searching my mind I said quickly, "Yes, I have met you,
but I can't remember where."

"A year ago," he replied. "I'm the man who came to your
back door and you gave me a sandwich. You may remember I had been to Detroit and was hitchhiking back to
Georgia. Things have changed for me since then. Now I'm a
member of a Baptist church in Atlanta, Georgia. In fact,

I'm even an assistant teacher in a men's class. As I came up the highway within thirty miles of your house tonight, I felt I had to see you again. You see, of all the people who gave me food and helped me on my way home, you were the only one who said you were glad you could do it for Christ's sake. When I left here I could not forget that you had emphasized that you were helping me because Christ had commanded it. I left your house that night with a warm feeling in my heart and a desire to know more about the teachings of Christ. I realized that if the teachings of Christ were that we show love to others as you showed it to me that night, then the whole world needed to know and to follow his teachings. When I got back home to Georgia I went to a church and accepted Christ as my Saviour. It was because of what you said that night that I am a Christian." Did it make any difference that my kindness was done in his name? It made all the difference, for because it was done in his name another man had become a Christian.

This is the fruit of a Christian.

Let us remember this truth also concerning rewards. God's response to our loving deeds in his name is not "pay." What is the difference between "pay" and rewards? When my wife was a little girl skating on her street she found a diamond ring. Her mother located the ad in the paper telling of the loss of the ring and offering a reward. Together they went to the address and immediately the owner identified it on the hand of June's mother. Eagerly and tearfully she pointed to the one of the three. She gave June three dollars reward. In those days that was quite a gift! If she had paid her for the deed one cent would have been adequate wages for picking up the ring. God does not pay wages, God rewards man—even for giving a cup of cold water in his name.

Many Christians excel in making investments that will produce great returns and yet they overlook the investment which yields the highest of all dividends. God has promised rewards, and rewards are always many times greater than the value of the actual investment. No other investment can approach one made in his name. If the standard used to measure is the percentage of return based on the capital invested then on the basis of return alone no investment can equal one made in the cause of our Lord. To follow his ordained plan is more to be sought after than great riches. "The ordinances of the Lord are true and righteous altogether. . . . In keeping them there is great reward" (Psalm 19:9–11, RSV). The returns for investment in his name are so fantastic that we are told, "Eye hath not seen, nor ear heard, neither have entered into the heart of man the things which God hath prepared for them that love him" (1 Cor. 2:9).

Another truth to consider about rewards is the fact that a person may be tricked, and thus lose them. "Let no man beguile you of your reward in a voluntary humility and worshipping of angels, intruding into those things which he hath not seen, vainly puffed up by his fleshly mind" (Col. 2:18). The method of bribery used on the Christian is a common one. A parent often uses the same method in bribing a baby to give up something he is holding which could be injurious to him. Of course, the parent could grab the scissors or knife from the baby's grip, but not without great protest and arousing rebellion. The wise parent instead tricks him out of them. He offers something to the baby colorful and attractive, getting him so interested in the substitute that he loses interest in the scissors or the other object, not realizing he is being tricked. The parent's act is a necessity for protection of the child. Satan, however, uses these tactics to the detriment of the Christian. He offers the Christian personal gain or pleasure, thus capturing his attention and interest. In the process the Christian is scarcely aware he is being tricked out of something much more precious than that being offered.

Consider also how the cares of the world and deceitfulness of riches have choked the Word. Accepting a small gain, he loses a great reward. The promise of our Lord in the Sermon on the Mount is that truly great rewards await him who can qualify. "But love ye your enemies, and do good, and lend, hoping for nothing again; and your reward shall be great, and ye shall be the children of the Highest" (Luke 6:35).

There is one other promise used in connection with rewards that has an unusual meaning to me personally. That phrase is, "In no wise shall he lose his reward." Simply stated it means that there is no condition possible under which a Christian can lose his reward. This means much to me, because as a high school boy I received one of the greatest disappointments of my life in failing to receive a reward many others had received under similar circumstances.

While clerking in a store one summer I was invited to go fishing with three men and another boy. It was quite evident that I was to be the companion of this man's nephew, a stranger to me. Arriving at the river the men went off in one direction, telling us to fish somewhere else. The men went quite a distance up the river bank and then circled back to fish from a small peninsula, actually only several hundred yards from us.

My companion and I were fishing from a boat anchored to the bank by a long chain. Bait, however, was scarce and the boy was losing bait so fast I knew it wouldn't last long. When I asked him to be more careful with the bait he stubbornly paid no heed. The fair way, I decided, was to divide the remaining bait in two cans. Then I climbed out on the bank and went a short way to fish.

No sooner had I put my bait in the water than I heard a big splash, and looking back I saw my companion had fallen into the water. To my horror he did not come up. Waiting a moment I saw he still had not come up. Calling in great fear and distress to the men across on the peninsula, I hurried down the muddy bank, slipping and falling, and getting up again to go on. By the time I reached the boat, it had drifted in a few feet toward the bank. I jumped from the bank into the boat, but as I landed I fell. But fortunately by pushing myself up, I could see over the side of the boat where he had gone down. However, the water was so murky I could see nothing but a slight discoloration some inches under the surface. No one can know the thrill I experienced when I reached for something that I did not even know was there and found my hands touching the boy's hair. I pulled him to the top and was able to get him halfway into the boat. Hanging half in and half out of the boat, he began coughing and his lungs began to clear of water. After a few minutes he sat up.

Shortly after this the men arrived, and we all hurried to the hospital. Suddenly I realized that I had saved a life!

Always I had dreamed of being a hero. As a boy scout I longed to earn a lifesaving badge. In fact, at that time there was really only one other thing I wanted—a 14-jewel gold watch. Just then the thought crossed my mind that this boy's father was a jeweler, and surely he would want to offer me a present.

Going back to the store I waited for things to happen. Most of all I was looking for someone from the newspaper to get the story. I waited and waited until noon came and passed. Late in the afternoon the boy's father came into the store and asked me to step outside where we could talk. Then he said, "I will never be able to tell you how much I owe you for saving my son's life today." With that statement the entire episode was closed. There was no news story. There was no lifesaving medal. Not even a gold watch. Often I have thought he could have tried to show me how much he appreciated it. As a boy I felt so deeply the loss of a reward that I felt should have been mine. But the years since then have brought a rich meaning and profit from the experience.

In closing this chapter may we underline the difference again between rewards and inheritance. A Christian receives an inheritance through the first cross on which another paid the price. To this the Christian may also add rewards to the inheritance by taking up the second cross, where he himself must be crucified unto the "world and the world unto him." If one is to gain rewards the two crosses must be kept in order—first, the foundation which is laid —the first cross—and upon this a worthy building which shall be built by accepting the second cross.

11.
"All Things Work Together for Good" Romans 8:28

Recently before the great battle of the two top football teams of the nation for the championship the news broke that the star quarterback had received an injury and might not play in the championship game. The attention of the sports-minded world was centered on this player. Every newspaper and sportscast was awaited eagerly. The coach, his staff and the doctors gave round-the-clock care and medical treatment. Perhaps no one in the entire United States was given more care and attention than that given the star quarterback.

But the protection received and the concern shown for him cannot approach that given by our Lord to one who is "in accord with his will." God has not only promised care and concern to this one but has given an almost unbelievable guarantee that the man in accord with his purpose shall ever live in a controlled situation. Unequivocably God states "that all things work together for good to the called in accord with his purpose" (cf. Rom. 8:28).

The most unreasonable man in the world is the man who goes out "on his own" and then blames God for what happens to him. Repeatedly God has pointed out that there is a place he has planned for every man, and if man is in that place God will bring even good out of his mistakes and the evil that is brought upon him.

God has a place and a plan for everything in his creation. He is not a God of haphazardness. He "hath made of one blood all nations of men for to dwell on all the face of the earth, and hath determined the times before appointed, and the bounds of their habitation" (Acts 17:26). He has a plan for all nations. He also has a plan and a purpose for every man, but only when that man lives in accord with God's plan. Then he lives in a controlled situation in a controlled world.

This is God's promise.

Since God promises this only to the man in accord with his purpose, then to discover his purpose is the highest goal attainable. No price is too great to pay for this knowledge. This, then, should be the greatest concern of every Christian.

Two calls of the Holy Spirit a man must answer in order to be in accord with God's will. First, he must accept the call of the Holy Spirit to accept Christ as his Saviour. Second, he must answer the Holy Spirit's call in permitting God's total purpose to be realized in his own life.

These two purposes God planned before the foundation of the world—that of sending his Son to atone for man's sin, and then man's becoming his instrument in reaching his fellowman with the good news of salvation. Any man whose life is not being used for others is a man in whom God's purposes are not being realized. He may be a Christian, but he cannot claim to be in accord with God's purpose for him.

> What does love look like?
> It has the hands to help others.
> It has the feet to hasten to the poor and needy.
> It has the eyes to see misery and want.
> It has the ears to hear the sighs and sorrows of men.
> That is what love looks like.
>
> St. Augustine (354–430)

For the man who is in accord with God's purpose, he has promised that all things will work together for good. Notice, God did not say that all things that happen to the Christian will be good. This would be impossible, for God has not created a robot. Man has a will. He will make choices which are not good. Many may even get hurt as a result of these choices. However, even then, God will still take a hand. And this intervention of God in the situation will bring good out of evil for those in accord with his purpose.

Again may we emphasize that the promise "for all things work together for good" is applicable only for those in accord with his purpose. This is illustrated in the parable of the vineyard that brought forth wild grapes. God's plan was for the vineyard to bring forth good grapes. "I will tell you what I will do to my vineyard: I will take away the hedge thereof, and it shall be eaten up; and break down the wall thereof, and it shall be trodden down: and I will lay it waste: it shall not be pruned, nor digged; but there shall come up briers and thorns: I will also command the clouds that they rain no rain upon it" (Isa. 5:5–6).

Notice the tower which was the sign of ownership was not torn down, but rather the fence and the hedge, the signs of special protection and care, were removed. What God had planned for a garden had become a desert.

One day while visiting a farm I noticed the cows in the corn patch. Rushing to the farmer I offered to help him remove the cattle. Instead of showing concern he nonchalantly said, "They're enjoying it, aren't they? Well, it doesn't matter. There isn't enough corn in that patch to even bother with. You see, the dry weather completely ruined the crop and yesterday I took down the fence."

Immediately my mind shifted to the Scripture of the vineyard. For God, like my farmer friend, had removed that special protection and care, because the vineyard as well as the cornfield had become unproductive. Applying this truth to a Christian we can say it would be foolish presumption for him to count on God's protection and care when he deliberately refuses to follow God's will.

Let me give an example.

Some years ago while I pastored a large city church on a busy boulevard my wife and I felt the necessity of making a safe place for our two-year-old daughter to play. The fence and the locked gate seemed adequate protection, until one day my wife rushed into the house, saying she had found a nail protruding from the fence. As soon as that was removed we both scoured that yard and fence for anything that would harm our daughter. Broken glass hidden in some of the taller grass was picked up piece by piece. Everything we could find that might harm her was removed. We did not go up the boulevard removing glass and nails, for we made safe the only place in which we wanted her to play.

God also has a safe place planned for each of his children who will live in accord with his will. Outside of that place man is on his own. The place God has planned is the land flowing with milk and honey. It is open only to the Christian who is willing to pay the price to attain it. For him the very door of heaven on earth swings wide.

In 1943, the Japanese shot down a *P-38* over the jungles of New Britain. The pilot, Fred Hargesheimer, has been sent to photograph enemy installations. Landing in the mud he quickly gathered up his parachute. Which way to go? Around him was a hundred miles of thick jungle, and even if he could reach the shore there would be 200 miles of open ocean between him and the Allied-held New Guinea. Aside from the Japanese the only inhabitants of the island were primitive Melanesians, spear-carrying Stone Age people.

After struggling for ten days through underbrush he reached an abandoned lean-to. Here he ate roots and snails and built a crude cross. As he knelt there daily he found strength in the words of the twenty-third Psalm. "He leadeth me beside the still waters . . . Thou preparest a table before me in the presence of mine enemies."

Thirty-one days later he was discovered and rescued by some Melanesian Christians. At the risk of their lives, there at Nantambu he was protected from the Japanese. When he came down with malaria and was sure he would die, Ida, who was nursing her baby, came each day and gave him a cup of milk from her own breast. This saved his life. Nine months later these natives helped him escape (Fred Hargesheimer, *"Why I Can't Forget Nantambu," Guideposts Magazine,* Nov. 1965, pp. 12–14).

The Christian lives in a controlled situation with God at the controls when that person is in accord with God's purpose.

12.
The Acceptable Sacrifice
Romans 12

If life is a journey then one may find a reliable travel brochure in Romans 9–12. In these chapters Paul describes a journey which is God's will that every man should make, a journey to be made in two stages—from the death sentence into life and from life into the Land of Promise. Escape from the death sentence into life is the theme of chapters 8–10. The second part of the journey from the desert into the Promised Land is the theme of chapter 12.

As one stands with Paul at Romans 12:1 he has finished a part of the journey. He may look two ways—*back* to the part completed and *ahead* to the second part which Paul is urging him now to begin. There is no other place in all the writings of Paul where such a detailed brochure is given. Here the span from death to life is an accomplished fact. The cost for this part of the journey has been paid by another. The second part must be paid by the Christian himself. Paul's plea is: "I beseech you therefore, brethren, by the mercies of God, that ye present your bodies a living sacrifice." Here again it is evident that to complete *all* the journey which God intended for man involves two deaths.

The first has already been accomplished on the cross. The second is the voluntary death to self in the believer.

Paul leaves no question as to the high cost of this second part of the journey. In fact, the tremendous cost is the first fact to greet the eyes as one opens the brochure. There stands out in huge capitals on the first page—the death of self is the cost of this journey. The apostle knew that many would think this price was too high. This had been true of Demas, for Paul wrote: "Demas hath forsaken me, having loved this present world." His answer immediately to this is: "This is your *reasonable* service." Some translate this as "spiritual service." This might well be what Paul was emphasizing.

The early Christians in Rome were not masters but servants. They well understood the complete service a servant owed his master. His readers were those who were already servants and owed service to an earthly master. They also owed this submission of self as a spiritual service to him who had bought them as truly as they owed temporal service to an earthly master who also had bought them.

Not only did Paul insist on this offering of self as a reasonable service, but proclaimed the purchase of us by Christ an act of mercy. He reminded them that God did not pay this price for them because they were profitable servants, but out of mercy. "I beseech you . . . by the *mercies* of God, that ye present your bodies." The price they were asked to pay was no greater than the price another had already paid for them. The cost of both the first part of the journey completed and the part just ahead was a "body given or placed on the altar of sacrifice."

The ones to whom Paul addressed this well understood

the sacrifice of a body on the altar. Since the time of their deliverance from Egypt they had relived this hour and had been reminded again and again of the cost each time a sacrifice was placed on the altar. The Christian also understands the meaning of the body placed on the altar. He, too, comes again and again to relive the hour of his deliverance as he sees the broken body and the shed blood of our Lord. "This is my body, which is broken for you" (1 Cor. 11:24).

There was no doubt what Paul was asking of those who participated in the Passover supper, nor should there be any doubt in the minds of those of us who partake at the Lord's table. The request is clear. Because of God's mercy and because "God so loved the world, that he gave his only begotten Son" on the altar of the cross, man is asked to present his body on the altar as a return sacrifice. Giving to God a wholly yielded life may seem a tremendous and difficult choice to make, but thousands through the centuries have made it. Bill Borden, a wealthy young man, stood one day in Yale College and saw a friend pass by in a new sports car. Turning to another friend he said, "I wish I could afford a car like that!"

"Why, Bill," said the astonished friend, "you could buy several cars like that."

"No," replied Bill, "I can't afford it." But at that very time he was spending thousands for missions in the city where he attended college. He had heeded this call from Christ to present his all to him as a sacrifice.

A return look at the cross, Paul knew, would renew the former experience of joy. "Be ye transformed by the *renewing of your mind*." In essence Paul is asking the Christian to reserve his judgment concerning the cost until he reviews his experience at the cross. To be sure, this should happen each time the Christian partakes of the Lord's Supper. It is imperative to note this is a *renewal,* an experience that is only possible because it has happened at a prior time. For example, a magazine cannot be renewed until it has been ordered at least once before. Thus, Paul is writing to the man who has already shared in the experience of the cross at a former time, the moment of his acceptance of Christ as Saviour. To come and stand again before the cross has through the centuries settled the matter for many. They turn from the cross with hearts crying out as did Isaac Watts:

> When I survey the wondrous cross,
>   On which the Prince of glory died,
> My richest gain I count but loss,
>   And pour contempt on all my pride.

A trip back to the cross, Paul knew, would also bring about the offering of self in the only manner acceptable unto God.

This offering of the body to Christ remains valueless unless prompted by *love.* Notice Paul does not say, "I command you to *pay,* but I beseech you to *present,* because of the mercy of God to you."

It was this gift of herself that Miss Ettie Lee, a Los Angeles high school teacher gave. Seeing so many of her brightest students becoming dropouts, she asked God what she could do about it. The answer revealed to her was the establishment of home ranches where they would receive love and direction toward God. Of course, this could not come to pass on a teacher's salary, so she learned the real estate business. Today her wealth is more than three million dollars, with an income of some $125,000 going to support the Ettie Lee Homes, Inc., a nonprofit corporation operating 14 ranches for the rehabilitation of "incorrigible" boys, many from broken homes. But for her love and understanding these hundreds of boys would have been lost from themselves, lost from God and society.[1]

Continuing the parallel between a brochure of a journey and Romans 12, one will be shocked by the glaring differences between them. There is no picture of a beautiful scene on the front page, no catch phrase, nothing but the cold facts standing out in bold, stark reality. "The Cost of This Journey Is the Death of Self." Paul states this first, because unless one is prepared to make this step, he is only passing away his time in reading what follows. Should the reader reply that the cost is too great, Paul would remind him of those who have taken that journey. A chorus from every age and country would gladly testify, "For him I have suffered the loss of all things—and count them as nothing!" That which I have given fades away into nothing when compared to that which I have gained. Morris L. West voiced this eloquently in his powerful novel *The Tower of Babel:* "At the center of every self was a walled area which the self would defend like a sacred stone. The mystics of every faith knew that the moment of peace came when this wall was torn down and the self was renounced." [2]

In verse 1 Paul established the price of the journey as the sacrifice of self. The power to accomplish this will come from a return visit to the cross. The reason for this is that you "may prove what is the good, perfect, and acceptable will of God." The purpose for which a Christian should make a total commitment is quite evident. There is no

greater achievent possible for men than that promised by
Paul that through the dedicated Christian God will show
the world what his will is as revealed in a surrendered
believer. It is reported [3] that D. L. Moody once heard
someone say, "The world has yet to see what God can do
with, and for, and through, and in a man who is fully and
wholly consecrated to Him." Moody said, "I will try my
utmost to be that man." His influence has girdled the globe
many times and has touched millions. Is it possible that a
Christian would draw back from a total surrender to the
will of God if he understood that the bridge between God
and man is constructed only from surrendered lives?

A Christian's love must reach out in two directions—
back to the cross and out to the world. The looking back
will renew the mind. The looking out to the needs of the
world must be followed by man's answer to God, "Thy will
be done." To be a part in bridging the chasm between God
and man is that which God purposes for every man who
knows him. This is Paul's meaning when he states: "That ye
may prove what is that good, and acceptable, and perfect
will of God."

Too frequently we hear the statement, "If *he* is a Christian, I have no desire to be one!" And again, "If that is all
that Christianity or Christ can do for a man then I am just
as well off without him." But what is actually accomplished
in most Christian lives is not nearly all that Christ can do
for a man. God is asking man to present himself to him that
he might *prove,* or show, what is his good, and acceptable,
and perfect will.

A man once mentioned to his contractor friend that he
would like to have his house remodeled. In following the

directions given for locating the house his friend had already remodeled, he mistook it for another. Meeting his contractor friend later he was asked, "How did you like the house I remodeled?"

"I didn't like it at all!"

Knowing there was some mistake the contractor took him to the house he had remodeled. His friend exclaimed, "This is not the one I looked at. It was another."

His friend smiled and replied, "That is the house of a man who has never let me work on it." Thousands of Christians have not permitted the Master Contractor to fashion their lives into his good, perfect, and acceptable will. Consequently, the world has no vision of God's will of what a man or woman should be in his plan.

There is also the error in thinking that the moment a life is surrendered to the Lord that his will is done completely in it. However, the moment the surrender is made the work begins in it. This could be illustrated by the instance of a man buying a piece of property. As he views his purchase he sees many changes he would like to make. Perhaps he would like to tear down certain partitions or sections and put in others. On a farm he might plan to replace the tumbledown barn with a modern efficient dairy barn. Of course, this work could not be accomplished in a moment. The changes the owner has visualized can come about only when the old has been replaced by the new. *But there must come a moment before any of this renovation can take place—when the title is surrendered to him.* Isn't this exactly the plea of Paul? Present your bodies to him. Turn over the title to the Great Architect that he may begin to make that life according to his specifications.

What a blessed and refreshing experience it is to see the will of God worked out in the life of a believer! In the early Christian centuries Cyprian wrote to his friend, Bonatus: "We are living in a bad world, an incredibly bad world, but there is living among us a quiet and holy people, who though they suffer, yet have faith. They are masters of their souls. They are called Christians and I have become one of them."

One cannot leave this verse without noting that only by the yielding of one's will, oneself or ego, can the will of God be perfected in that individual. Any life without such a committal can only be compared to an incompleted house or an unfinished journey.

Notes

1. "Empire," Denver *Post*, November 7, 1965.
2. Morris L. West, *Tower of Babel* (William Morrow, 1968), p. 72.
3. Paul D. Moody and A. P. Fitt, *The Shorter Life of D. L. Moody* (Chicago: Bible Colportage Assoc., c 1900).

13.
Thinking Straight

We often miss God's message either because we are not listening or because we are not thinking straight. Many years ago in the early days of the Morse code a newspaper advertised for a telegrapher. A young man joined a roomful of applicants and began listening to the dots and dashes. He walked without hesitation into the inner office. In a few minutes he came out saying, "Well, people, you can leave now. I've got the job."

Not understanding, someone spoke up, "But we were here first."

"But weren't you listening? The dots and dashes were saying if you can understand these dots and dashes, come in. The first one in gets the job."

The message of God in Romans is: "This is the will of God." In Romans 12 Paul declares that the will of God is a perfected (completed) product. He also states that the will of God is acceptable. Although many do not reject the fact that the will of God is good and perfect, they are still reluctant to believe that it is acceptable or practical for them in their present situation.

Why do many today hear the plea for consecration and yet turn away from it? Perhaps for the same reason as some of Christ's followers. They said, "This is an hard saying; who can hear it?" (John 6:60). The same thought is echoed in Paul's writing in this chapter when he declares that some believers will reject God's will as unacceptable. Not willing to pay the price, they may be thinking, "It is just too much to give up. It is too stringent." Anticipating this attitude, Paul continues in Romans 12:3, "I say . . . to every man that is among you, not to think of himself more highly than he ought to think; but to think soberly."

For just a moment let us ask this question, "What do we possess today?" Is it material goods of this earth? How did we acquire them? Perhaps we reply, "Through our own labors." Then who gave us the health to enable us to labor? God. Who gave us the keen mind for success? God. "What hast thou that thou didst not receive? now if thou didst receive it, why dost thou glory, as if thou hadst not received it?" (1 Cor. 4:7). Is there anyone who can honestly say he has too much to give up? We have nothing except what God bestows upon us.

Sometime ago I saw a man staggering along the street. An officer, thinking he was drunk, stopped him. Tests revealed no alcohol on his breath. He was acting drunk because of a blow on the head. The word "drunk" could be translated "having the mind blinded, under another's influence, a blurring of the senses and mind." Isn't that just what God is saying in this verse: "Be not drunk on your possessions or even on yourself, but be sober—think soberly." Too many Christians today have become intoxicated on the things of this world. "The care of this world, and the deceitfulness of riches, choke the word" (Matt. 13:22), crowding it out and blinding the mind.

The truth of God's claim for surrender has not been widely recognized in the Christian world. The consequences can be seen all around us in unfruitful, empty, unfulfilled lives. The vast multitudes of lost people have seen few rays of light from the great numbers of professing Christians. Let no man be drunk on these things, but think soberly, "according as God hath dealt to every man the measure of faith" (Rom. 12:3).

What is the meaning of "measure of faith"? Does God deal out a certain amount of faith? No, our amount of faith is dependent upon us, and not upon God. In accordance with the measure God gives for faith, you have received salvation free. God metes out to us salvation because of our faith, not because of our merit. Thus, Paul is reminding us that even our salvation was meted out to us because of our faith. This should humble even the proudest. This gripped the heart of Isaac Watts when he wrote:

> Forbid it, Lord, that I should boast,
>   Save in the death of Christ my God;
> All the vain things that charm me most,
>   I sacrifice them to His blood.

Besides the group of Christians who think too much of themselves there is another group who think too little of themselves. To them the apostle says, "For as we have many members in one body, and all members have not the same office: so we, being many, are one body in Christ, and every one members one of another" (Rom. 12:4–5). That we are all members of the body of Christ is enough to convince us of the value of even the smallest member. How forcefully this truth is presented in 1 Corinthians 12:18,22: "Now hath God set the members every one of them in the body, as it hath pleased him. Nay, much more those members of the body, which seem to be more feeble, are necessary."

A visit to any hospital would draw our attention to the fact that very few, if any, patients are there because *all* their members are sick. Perhaps it is an ailing liver, appendix, or gall bladder. Whatever the disorder it took only one ailing member to make the rest of the body sick. How important that each member, though small, be strong!

Often the smallest part of a machine makes possible the movement of a larger part. Without the wrist the agility of the hand would certainly be lessened. In a church it is often an obscure person who makes possible even the work of the minister. At one time in the author's ministry there was such a deacon. No one would have thought God could do much through him. His talents were few, but his words of confidence and encouragement to a young preacher gave that young minister courage in a dark hour.

Our Lord delights in taking little things and doing great things with them. It was only three loaves and five fishes he used to feed five thousand. It was only a rod in Moses' hand which divided the water. It was only a sling and a stone in the hand of David that he used to kill Goliath. It was only a raven God used in feeding his servant Elijah. It was only three hundred pitchers and lamps held by three hundred dedicated, unified, obedient men that a great army was put to flight. It is not what we surrender to the Lord as much as what he can do with it. "I beseech you by the mercies of God to present your bodies a living sacrifice"—that he may prove what he can do with it. Today he is saying to us, as he did to Moses, "What is that in thy hand? Will you not give it to me that I may use it mightily?"

Were it possible for us to use a telescope to pierce the distant future we might be amazed to see some wearing crowns who seemed to make very little dent in this world and yet who had proved faithful with the few talents given them. Some years ago in New York City there lived a humble scrubwoman named Annie. Uneducated in books, she was well educated with her Saviour. Into the wealthiest homes of the city this humble disciple went with her witnessing. When employers tried to curb her testimony she would smilingly reply, "No preach, no scrub!" When she died several hundred New Yorkers passed by her casket in loving tribute, among them doctors, lawyers, and businessmen whom she had won to the Saviour.

Continuing our theme concerning the journey to the Promised Land let us note that the believers Paul addressed in Romans 12 were standing at the same crossroads at which the Israelites of old stood. Without violating the truth of his words, I believe we could freely translate Paul's admonition to hesitating Christians: You say the price is too great? I ask you to go back to the cross and see anew the price Christ paid for your sonship to God. You say you have too much to give? Let no man think of himself more highly than he ought to think, but let him think soberly (v. 3). You say you have so little that what you do makes little difference? What you do is of utmost importance. You are a part of Christ. You say people don't live that way today? God answers, "Be not conformed to this world." The cost of your refusal is too great both to yourself and to the world. For your loss will be peace, joy, and fulfilment. The loss to the world will be the proof that God's will is good, perfect, and acceptable for all men.

In every age God has provided spiritual giants, God-possessed men and women to stand out as markers for a better life. In our own century Kagawa was one of those. Born the illegitimate son of a geisha girl and a prominent businessman, he longed to learn the English language. Permission was given for him to attend classes given by Dr. Myers, a Presbyterian missionary in Japan. As the students read the New Testament they came to the crucifixion. Deeply moved, Kagawa asked, "Why did they do this to such a good man? Why did he let them?"

"Because," said the missionary, "He loved man so much he was willing to die that man should find God."

Without a word Kagawa dashed from the room, running until he could find a quiet place. Then falling on his knees he cried, "Oh, God, make me like Christ!"

In the years that followed God answered that prayer. His life touched millions in the slums; his witness for Christ as a preacher and a writer have touched the world.

14.
Equal in Service

All sorts of avenues are being traveled in order to find answers for today's living—from the hippies and flower children to meditation as represented by the teaching of the Indian mystic Maharishi Mahesh (Yogi). Long ago Paul gave the answer that will solve this problem and quest for the twentieth century as well as for the first: "I beseech you therefore, brethren, by the mercies of God, that ye present your bodies a living sacrifice, holy, acceptable unto God, which is your reasonable service" (Rom. 12:1).

No other fact needs more emphasis than this—that the consecration or discipleship to which God calls a man is a very practical thing. In some instances it has been made so impractical that many have turned from it. It has been pictured often only in the realm of a church-related vocation. What a tragedy if all Christians were to become full-time vocational church workers, leaving their professional, business, and homelife pursuits for the pulpit! Where would be the listeners? In the mind of God every believer is a member of the body which carries out his plan, but in many different places and professions.

An illustration from nature shows how God so wisely works all things together for good. Oysters living in the North Sea require an immense supply of lime to form shells. Where does this vast supply of lime come from? It is brought down every year by the Rhine from the Alps. In order to produce this lime, the sun, through its great power, lifts water from the ocean to form clouds. In turn the clouds fall in the form of snow upon the mountains. Then the snow is turned into ice and becomes a glacier. The glacier grinds and pulverizes the granite rocks into lime, and the Rhine River carries the lime to the North Sea, where the oysters make use of it in growing shells. Thus, all the forces of nature cooperate to help a tiny oyster grow. If God provides so carefully for one of his smallest creatures, how confident we should be that he has planned as thoughtfully his work in his church, each talent needed in its place of service.

In this chapter Paul mentions several areas of service. First, if a man is given the gift to prophesy, then let him preach. If his talent is ministry, then let him minister or serve. Frequently the word "ministry" refers to the work of deacons. Alongside these gifts is that of teaching. From the text we can see there is no less compulsion laid upon him to teach than there is upon the prophet to prophesy. If he is teaching, he is doing as fully the will of God as that of the preacher or deacon.

Some Christians have wondered about the work of the next talent mentioned—the exhorter. He is the one who stimulates other believers to action, who rouses and inspires them for service for Christ. His job is to encourage others to do more for God. He could be the president or officer of a class, a group leader in the church or Christian organization. In the sight of the Great Husbandman the work of the exhorter is as important as that of the prophet.

The next person commended is he that *giveth*. If that is his talent, then let him use it for God. In a small town there was a ramshackle store, run-down, unattractive. Its owner seemed to match his store, for he was slovenly and careless in his own appearance.

One day the citizens of the community noticed a new sign over his store—"Pam Chick and Partner." Immediately things changed. Windows were cleaned and new displays arranged in them. Shelves were rearranged with shining new stock. The owner put on a new suit of clothes. There seemed to be a total remodeling job of both the store and the owner. Often people asked, "Who is the new partner?" But no one found out until years later. When Pam Chick died the books were opened, and at the heading of the accounts were these words—"Pam Chick and Jesus Christ." His change indicated his knowledge of the truth that partnership with Jesus Christ involves not only cleaning up but sharing all with the partner. "Whatsoever ye do in word or deed, do all" to the glory of God. (Col. 3:17) Too often the churches have emphasized giving money as the greatest talent. But the Master who gives the gifts recognizes no gift above another. The faithful giver has his place in the plan of God as truly as the teacher, preacher, and deacon.

Another talent mentioned is that of "ruling." Perhaps we have put our rulers as the most outstanding members of our churches. That is not the Master's order. All are on the same level. If a man has the gift to rule, then let him rule as a Christian. Since there were no rulers in the church, Paul has reference here to those who rule in society.

Along with and equal to the talents mentioned of preaching, ministering, teaching, giving, and ruling, Paul mentions
the humble talent of showing mercy. What might that in-
volve? All of life, really—visiting the sick, helping those in
distress, showing loving-kindness in a multitude of ways. We
must note that the one qualification tagged to this gift is that
the one showing mercy shall do it with cheerfulness, not
grudgingly or as a matter of duty. That attitude of service is
not acceptable to God.

Let us notice the qualities God associates with gifts. If a
man shows mercy, let him be cheerful. If a man be a ruler,
let him be diligent. If a man give, let him do it with simplic-
ity or humility—not with a fanfare of publicity.

What a tragedy for a church when one of the members
fails to use his talent! God's work will go on, but the teaching
may have to be done by an exhorter, or the giving may not
be done. It is difficult to believe that God ever had any job
and no one to fill it. It is easier to believe that someone
either was not prepared for the work or was unwilling to
accept it. The greatest challenge—and fulfilment—facing
Christians is to find the mission God has for him.

God delights in doing great things with little things. God
does not need much of a man, according to man's stand-
ards, but he does need all of that man. Every man is
measured by a standard according to his talents. "For unto
whomsoever much is given, of him shall be much required:
and to whom men have committed much, of him they will
ask the more" (Luke 12:48).

For example, God may give ten talents to one man, but if
that man uses only five God ranks him on the basis of ten,
and his rating is thus only 50 percent. To another who

receives only two talents from God, but uses them for his Master, there will be a ranking of 100 percent in the eyes of God. In comparing the two, man probably would rate the man using five but having ten talents higher than the man having two, and using two. But God would appraise them this way: "Many that are first shall be last; and the last shall be first" (Matt. 19:30). The most talented Christian should be the most concerned and humble lest he neglect to use even one of the talents God has given him. Above all he should remember, "What hast thou that thou didst not receive? now if thou didst receive it, why dost thou glory, as if thou hadst not received it?" (1 Cor. 4:7).

One should not overvalue himself, even though he be a great orator or teacher for God, for it is possible at the same time that he could be a hindrance to the spread of the gospel. By not giving his all he could be preventing another who would give his all in filling the place already occupied. In spite of the warning God has given us in the Bible we still will be surprised in the judgment to find many who were last down here brought to the front and given a place of honor in heaven. Many a quiet, unobtrusive, almost unnoticed Christian who has served God faithfully will be chosen from the crowd and given a chief place, while some with many talents who seem to shine so brightly today, using only a portion of their talents, will be unnoticed in that heavenly crowd.

In my thinking Mary will be one of those sitting closest to the Lord. This is a part of her story. One Sunday after I had preached on Romans 12, she said, "I never fully understood what it meant to present one's body as a living sacrifice. Please meet me in the morning, for I want to learn more." The next day in my study she placed in my hands $2,500 with this remark, "Use this money for the Lord for any cause that will honor him most." Some months later she came to the office again and placed in my hands another $2,500 to be used under the same conditions. That money was used to start three missions. Today those three missions are thriving churches. It was also used in starting a youth center in another city. Some of Mary's money also helped to educate a young missionary who today is serving in Japan. Her gifts did all that—and more. Her devout life has been an inspiration to her children, her community, and her many pastors. On earth she may not be well known, but in heaven she will wear a crown. Many in her church might ask, "Who is that?" But that question will not be asked in heaven, for she is listed in God's "Who's Who."

Paul's plea is the same—to the ten-talent person or to the one-talent person: "I beseech you therefore, brethren, by the mercies of God, that ye present your bodies a living sacrifice, holy, acceptable unto God, which is your reasonable service. And be not conformed to this world: but be ye transformed by the renewing of your mind, that ye may prove what is that good, and acceptable, and perfect, will of God."

15.
"And Having Done All to Stand"

Recently in successive newscasts and releases there came to United States citizens the running account of our armed forces in Vietnam as they tried to capture and hold hill 707. The most satisfying and significant newscast of all, and the one for which the whole nation waited, was given in only eight words, "We have made a stand at the top." So much was said in so few words. This statement announced to the world that not only had the United States troops captured the top of the hill but they had consolidated this position and repelled all enemy attacks to dislodge them. In fact, they had reached the top and for the first time had not been driven back down the hill. For the first time they had been able to make a stand.

Paul's concern for the Christians as he bade them farewell in his letter to the Ephesians was that they, too, having reached the plateau might be able to make a stand. Too many Christians in our own day spend much time battling to gain again the higher level only to retreat down the slope. Sad as it is to witness a believer in retreat from the heights, it is even sadder to see one who has given up the attempt to gain that higher level which God intended for him. In the words of Tennyson, "Tis better to have loved and lost than never to have loved at all."

Throughout his writings Paul makes it clear again and again that there is a plane higher than that on which the average Christian lives. In Ephesians 6:10 he states that three things are necessary if one is to make a stand after having gained that plateau.

First, any man can successfully make a stand at the top, but no man can do it in his own strength. This he reveals in the statement, "Be ye *made* powerful" (Eph. 6:10, RSV). Second, he emphasizes the danger of underestimating the power of the opposing forces. "For we wrestle not against flesh and blood but against principalities, against powers, . . . against spiritual wickedness in high places" (v. 12). Third, he goes into detail and at great length deals with the armor man must put on if he is to stand. Especially he urges that no part may be omitted. Not one of the above facts can be ignored if man is to hold the heights after having once gained them.

Concerning the first fact, that no man can stand in his own strength against the counterattacks, Paul stated unequivocally that man can *be made* powerful enough to stand —but only in the power of the Lord and his might. One of the miracles of the surrendered Christian life is the power of God flowing through him. But God reserves that power only for those who are willing to become the channel through which his power can flow, thus bringing light to overcome darkness. The darkness has never been able to hold back the light. Neither can the light be held back when God's power has a human channel to man.

Paul is thus saying to every Christian, "You can be made powerful." God's might can become so great in man that spiritual wickedness in high places can be overcome, if one is willing to be made powerful.

Next Paul leaves no doubt concerning the utter defeat man faces if he joins battle with the opposing forces while underestimating the power aligned against him. "For we wrestle not against flesh and blood, but . . . against spiritual wickedness in high places." The battle is actually against him who is next in power unto God. Even Michael, archangel, dared not bring a railing accusation against the devil, but said, "May the Lord rebuke thee." Failure to recognize the strength of the enemy has brought defeat to many a young Christian who has advanced into battle in his own strength. Some return from this first battle in defeat but also much wiser and with a new respect for the enemy and a greater dependence upon God. Others return from their defeat with no courage to try to gain the heights again.

One of the greatest fighters of all time, possibly even the greatest, was defending his title against the challenger (a smaller opponent). As I listened to a broadcast of this fight in the late rounds, to my utter surprise, the announcer said, "It looks like the champion is whipped! He is on the ropes!" Then to my even greater surprise he announced, "Wait a minute! The challenger, not the champ, is down. The champ has won again!" To the amazement of the sports-minded world the champ, apparently going down in defeat, had by one blow turned defeat into victory.

Some years later in an interview a sportscaster talking to the champ asked him this question, "What happened in the ring that night when the challenger apparently had you defeated, and then you were able to land one blow knocking him out?"

The answer of the champ was historic, for he replied, "The challenger underestimated the strength I had left, and he let his defense down."

In the strongest words possible Paul warns the Christian never to let down his defense, and above all, never to underestimate the power of the opponent—even when the victory appears already won. Every Christian would do well to become better acquainted with the devil in the sense that Paul attempts to reveal him to man. Our Lord himself also warned man against lack of respect for the powers against us. "Fear not them which kill the body, . . . but rather fear him which is able to destroy both body and soul in hell" (Matt. 10:28). In this Epistle to the Ephesians Paul underlines man's helplessness alone, but he also points to the great power of God to which he can connect. He describes the defenses which man must erect on the heights if he is to make a stand there.

These defenses Paul compares to parts of armor one must wear into battle, singling out certain parts of the body where man is especially vulnerable. One will miss some of the greatest truths here unless he realizes that the part of the body protected is the key to understanding this Scripture and that the part of the body to be protected is more important than the part of the armor that protects it.

The real meaning of this passage did not open for me until I paused one day to ask why Paul specified certain parts of the body to be protected by specific parts of the armor. Was there any special meaning in this, and if so, what was the meaning? Why were parts of the armor matched with certain parts of the body? For example, did Paul have a special purpose in pointing out that the *loins* must be girded about with truth, the *breast* or *chest* armor must be righteousness, and the *feet* must be shod with the gospel of peace.

In the understanding of the relationship between the part of the armor and the part of the body it protects there is found not only great spiritual truth which will enable man to stand but there is also revealed the most powerful prescription for physical health known to man.

What then is revealed to man through understanding the relation between the loins and the armor of truth which protects the loins? The loins are the *secret parts* of man, the organs hidden from the eyes of others. The apostle reveals here a great truth upon which both Christianity and psychiatry are based. "Let the hidden things in your life be truth." Do not permit anything to become a part of your life which you fear others might discover. Fear of discovery of some hidden thing can not only destroy peace but also health.

Modern psychiatry and Christianity advance hand in hand against one of the most devastating evils of this hour —FEAR, a power that is taking an unprecedented toll in peace, health, and even life itself. The cost of unnecessary fear, even in its toll in life, is beyond belief. On every side the following illustrations are multiplied, and in every community fear takes its terrible toll.

A man unable to hold his job and fearing for the future and welfare of his family guides his car off the highway into a tree or a bridge abutment.

A leader in his community facing discovery of embezzlement and fearing its discovery by others dies of self-inflicted wounds or carbon monoxide.

The young couple fearing discovery of their indiscretion join in a suicide pact.

The successful man fearing an unsuccessful future financially and in fear of what others will say chooses death as an alternative to facing that future. The epitaph for all these and thousands of others if truthfully written would be, "Here lies another victim of fear." One message needs to be emblazoned across the pages of every newspaper, spread on the screen of every television, and constantly proclaimed from every pulpit and radio, "Let your loins be girded about with truth."

The cost of any gain or any goal reached will be too great, if the making of that gain or the reaching of that goal carries with it a fear of discovery. The man who can go to his rest each night and rise to face the world each morning with peace in his own heart and goodwill toward man has secured for himself the most blessed riches this world can offer. Fear of discovery and the keeping up of a false front are the greatest destroyers of mankind.

No better philosophy was ever written than that voiced by the famous consumer of spinach, the comic strip character Popeye. In his simple and yet profound statement he states a philosophy that in itself would bring many to health. "I yam what I yam." This inscription if placed on the wall of the physician's office or in the counseling room of the minister, if read and adopted as the philosophy of the patient could terminate the visits of many seeking help for their personal problems.

I remember a social leader in a community where I

served as pastor. Her husband, a friend of mine, stopped me on the street one day. Although he was not a member of my church, his distress prompted him to ask my advice about sending his wife to an institution for special treatment. He explained she could not sleep at night, that she would walk the floor at night and even become incoherent while speaking.

I felt incompetent to give advice, but I did promise I would ask God to give him guidance in this urgent decision. Later that day I passed this friend's house and saw his wife sitting on the porch. God prompted me to ask if I could talk with her a few minutes. She was both gracious and grateful. After a few minutes I asked her a question I cannot ever remember asking before, "What are you afraid of?"

Indignantly she turned to me replying, "Why, I'm not afraid of anything! What made you ask that?" Somewhat apologetically I explained that a person hiding a fear often undergoes just such an experience as she was having. In a moment she looked up and through tears said, "Yes, I am afraid." Like so many fears we carry, hers was ridiculous. She explained that ever since she had moved to this community many years ago, she had been afraid that the acknowledged leader of the social life in the community would find out about her humble background. Hers had been a poverty-stricken home. In fact, she had never ridden in a car until after she married. Her family traveled to town in a mule-driven wagon. To her this seemed an especially degrading experience. With a new force in her voice she said, "I would rather die than have old Mrs. Brown know about that wagon and mule!"

There was no doubt in my mind now concerning the

advice I should give her. "You must go this very afternoon and tell Mrs. Brown about your humble home and the mule and the wagon." At first she rejected this counsel until I convinced her that not only was her peace of mind at stake but also her health. Only then did she agree to go, and that afternoon she brought her fear out into the open. She herself told Mrs. Brown what she had been afraid others might tell her. To her utter surprise Mrs. Brown replied that she, too, came from a humble home and that a person was far more important than the background from which she came. A mutual respect, and even affection, was born between these two women.

My friend stopped me on the street a few days later and told me that his wife had been healed almost miraculously and that she had again taken up all her community and church activities. I could not tell him about the prescription I had given her, because she had asked me not to reveal her fear to her husband. Unless she has told him he does not know until this day. However, I have often thought that if her future progress equaled her beginning progress she and her husband probably had a good laugh over it. When the loins are girt about with truth, fear finds little soil in which to grow.

Psychiatry says, "Bring your fears out into the open." Jesus said, "For there is nothing covered, that shall not be revealed, neither hid, that shall not be known" (Luke 12:2). Paul said, "have your loins girt about with truth."

An equally important truth is revealed by the next part of the body mentioned—the chest or breast. The armor designated for its protection is righteousness. As the loins are the most secret parts of the body so the chest is the exact opposite, for it is the most prominent, the first seen. We wear our flowers in our button holes and our pins in our lapels. When we want to describe one who pushes himself into the public eye, we say he is a "chesty" sort of individual. Thus when Paul writes, "Put on the breastplate of righteousness" he is saying that when others look at a Christian they should see one who believes in righteousness and is willing to let any man know where he stands. The believer who refuses to take a stand and who refuses to put on the breastplate of righteousness is constantly in trouble.

It is not the girl who makes it clear where she stands who must reject the advances of her date, but the one who leaves doubt as to where she stands. It is not the young man who makes it clear that he does not drink that is constantly bombarded with offers of drink, but the one who does not make his stand clear.

When I see a Christian attempting to straddle the fence, I remember an apple tree whose branches hung on both sides of a fence that separated a garden from a highway. Each day as the boys in our community walked home from school we passed this tree—and we were always hungry. The tree trunk was actually inside the fence which was nailed to it, but the branches spread over the grass on the roadside. We knew that any fruit that grew on the branches overhanging the road was fair game. We could only estimate where the fence would have divided the top of the tree, and our judgment in this respect I am sure cost the dear woman who owned the tree many apples. But her situation was even more to be deplored, because she never ate a ripe apple from that tree, and neither did we. In fact, we all started after the apples the moment they began to turn red. That unfortunate tree was beaten and shaken. Sometimes the limbs were broken by sticks we used to dislodge the apples before they were ready to fall. The buffeting and trials that tree suffered could have been avoided largely, if that tree had been on either side of that fence.

A Christian, too, will find the trials and troubles are many for him who tries to live on the border line and tries to reach out in both directions. When one fails to put on the breastplace of righteousness he is indeed asking for trouble. Jesus said, "Let your yea be yea; and your nay, nay; lest ye fall into condemnation" (James 5:12). The modern therapist would recommend that for peace a man must assess the situation and take a stand one way or the other. James also said, "He that wavereth is like a wave of the sea driven with the wind and tossed. A double minded man is unstable in all his ways" (1:6,8). No place is as difficult as astraddle the fence. If one is to stand, he must be able to make a decision and take a stand on his decision.

A third part of the body mentioned by Paul as important in making a stand is the feet. These, he points out, must be shod with the preparation of the gospel of peace. The feet, of course, symbolize the daily journey we make. Paul is thus saying, Let the day's work be that of helping to bring God's will to pass on earth through giving the message of peace to all men. This message is twofold: (1) peace with God through his cross, and (2) peace within for him who has found the second cross. The man whose feet are shod with the gospel of peace serves both God and man and in serving gains strength whereby he himself is able to stand.

The modern therapist would recommend that for health and peace a man must keep busy, be involved in some project or cause—occupational therapy. Jesus said, "He that giveth his life shall keep it." Paul said, Let your feet be "shod with the preparation of the gospel of peace" (Eph. 6:15).

It is almost startling to read the phrase in which the apostle describes the fourth part of the body and its protection, for he uses the phrase "above all." Emphatically he states, in effect: Now what I am about to say is even more important than the loins being girt about with truth, the breastplate of righteousness and the feet shod with the preparation of the gospel of peace. I am saying to you, *above all* take the *shield of faith* wherewith ye shall be able to quench all the fiery darts of the wicked one.

It is *faith* alone in God, in man, and in tomorrow that is powerful enough to deflect the fiery darts that penetrate all other armor.

If a man loses his shield of faith, he is vulnerable to defeat and ultimately will be destroyed. Without faith, fear slips into rule, and worry supplants peace. The lack of faith in this hour has been the spawning ground for a generation of full-time worriers. Even though our possessions are greater than those of preceding generations, we spend more time worrying. It might even appear today that according to man's possessions so shall be his worries.

An acquaintance of mine met an old friend who had acquired wealth through the wise purchase of several businesses. He noticed that his friend who used to be cheerful and happy was now constantly preoccupied, nervous, and visibly unhappy. In love and deep concern he approached his unhappy friend and said, "Jim, it is too bad that you have accumulated so many things, for concern over them keeps you from enjoying even one evening any more. In fact, Jim, it is too bad that you own so many things, because apparently they now own you."

We worry today either because something has happened or because it didn't happen. We worry because something might happen or because we think it could still happen. We even worry sometimes because we can't remember what it was we intended to worry about.

> Said the Robin to the Sparrow,
>   "I should really like to know
> Why these anxious human beings
>   Rush about and worry so."
>
> Said the Sparrow to the Robin:
>   "Friend, I think that it must be
> That they have no heavenly Father
>   Such as cares for you and me."
>   ELIZABETH CHENEY

One morning at the breakfast table on the day my wife was to speak at an important missionary meeting, she turned to me in anxiety and said, "I'm scared!" Daily she had been teaching our children that we can trust God to care for us. Somehow our four-year-old son could not reconcile her fear with her teaching. Looking at her a moment he said, "What's the matter, Mommy? Isn't God still up there?" Tears filled her eyes and brimmed over as she put her arms around our son, "Yes, dear, Jesus is still here. For a moment I had forgotten, but now I'm not afraid any more."

Perhaps you know this story of a man who came to grips with worry. He determined he would set aside a certain time each week to worry, and at this time he would deal with them. He even bought what he called his "worry book." When he started to worry about something, instead of worrying, he wrote it down in his book to take up during his worry time. Then he could forget it until that time. His belief was that if anything is worth worrying about it is also important enough to give undivided attention to it. In fact, it is too important to be crowded into an already full schedule. His worry time was 3 o'clock on Sunday afternoon, and then he would go into his room alone and take out his worry book. Needless to say, he was surprised to find that 90 percent of his worries were already solved, and he hurriedly concluded his worrying by putting down the remaining 10 percent to be taken up at his next worrying session.

Psychiatry would sanction this practice. Quit running these worries over and over through your mind. Jesus said, "Seek ye first the kingdom of God, and his righteousness, and all these things shall be added unto you" (Matt. 6:33). Paul said, take "the shield of faith wherever ye shall be able to quench all the fiery darts" (Eph. 6:16). Before we leave this passage let us give special attention to two words that make the difference between success and failure. These words are "whole armor" with emphasis on whole, or every part.

All the miles of defense man can build will become useless when only one small section of the defense crumbles. Possibly the most formidable defense ever constructed by man, the Maginot Line between France and Germany, crumbled when a breach was made in it. After it was overrun, most of it still stood, miles and miles of it still bristling with the latest and most powerful weapons manned by trained soldiers. Miles of the most gigantic concrete and steel barricade ever erected by man still stood, but the barricade was valueless because a breach had been made in it, permitting the enemy to flow through and attack from the rear. Because it was vulnerable at *one* point, the whole fell. Many a gate that is left open by the Christian for a supposedly harmless visit back into the past has proved to be his Achilles' heel. Unfortunately for the Christian this gate never fails to swing both ways, and this type of activity by the Christian is the answer to the wedge for the adversary.

No more fitting words than those with which Paul closed his letter to the Ephesians could be found as a last word to Christians today, "Wherefore take unto you the whole armour of God, that ye may be able to withstand in the evil day, and having done all, to stand" (6:13).

16.
Peace Within

Is it not significant that the same proclamation from God came both at the beginning and the ending of Christ's ministry on earth? At his birth the angels proclaimed "Peace on earth, good will toward men" (Luke 2:14). No other message from heaven or from our Lord himself is as prominent as the message of peace. Why is so much importance attached to it? Surely the answer can be found in the fact that God began his creation in peace and will bring peace again to his world. God cannot and will not experience defeat.

In the Garden of Eden there was peace. As soon as sin entered peace came to an end. But God in his infinite mercy moved immediately to restore peace, both between heaven and earth and within the hearts of men. God will not leave unfinished that which he has begun. His will is that peace shall reign throughout the universe.

This peace must be realized, but at a tremendous cost, for it can come only through the death of both Christ and man. Only through the death of Christ himself can reconciliation be made, peace be restored between God and man.

Only through man's own death to self can he find peace within.

The way back to the Garden of Eden is possible only to him who has discovered the two crosses. The man who has made the complete journey back to the good land to which God wills for him will say with Paul, "God forbid that I should glory, save in the cross of our Lord Jesus Christ, by whom the world is crucified unto me, and I unto the world" (Gal. 6:14).

A further explanation of God's move to restore peace is found in 2 Corinthians 5:17–20: "Therefore if any man be in Christ, he is a new creature: old things are passed away; behold, all things are become new. And all things are of God, who hath reconciled us to himself by Jesus Christ, and hath given to us the ministry of reconciliation; to wit, that God was in Christ, reconciling the world unto himself, not imputing their trespasses unto them; and hath committed unto us the word of reconciliation."

But God has planned that man also must have a part in this restoration. He, too, must share the cross. That gratification of self which cost Adam and Eve their paradise must now be put on the cross, if man is to reenter that intimate fellowship with God.

The regaining of the kingdom of God and of peace is through the Holy Spirit. "For the Kingdom of God is not meat and drink; but righteousness, and peace, and joy in the Holy Ghost" (Rom. 14:17). "The fruit of the Spirit is love, joy, peace, longsuffering, gentlenes, . . . meekness" (Gal. 5:22–23).

To summarize, it is quite evident that the Holy Spirit points man to two crosses and two realizations of peace.

(1) He points to the cross of Calvary and through that cross to peace with God. (2) He points to the cross of self, and through that cross the attainment of peace within. The cross of Golgotha brings freedom from guilt. The cross of self brings freedom from fear. The cross of Calvary prepares man for death. The cross of self prepares man for life.

Psychiatry is helping man today achieve these two goals: freedom from guilt and freedom from fear. Let us compare the goals of psychiatry with those of God as presented in the Bible.

Psychiatry says to man	*God says to man*
(1) Get rid of your guilt.	"In him we have forgiveness of sins" (Eph. 1:7).
(2) Get rid of your fear.	"Perfect love casteth out fear" (1 John 4:18).
(3) Get lost in service to others.	"Whosoever will lose his life . . . shall save it" (Luke 9:24).

When a man properly relates himself to the two crosses in the Scriptures, he finds a peace that passes all understanding. But both crosses are difficult for man to accept.

The first cross is difficult for some to accept, for it staggers even the imagination of man that the Creator would die for the created in order that man and God could be reconciled. The second cross is also difficult to accept, because acceptance of this cross means man must reverse the manner of life now natural to him. Self on the throne must end, and self on the cross must begin. Although it is difficult to accept, it is only through the second cross that man can regain peace and thus realize the fulness of life God wills for him. The way lost by the one who enthrones self can be regained only by those who will crucify self. Only those who have been to the two crosses may say with Paul, "God forbid that I should glory, save in the cross of our Lord Jesus Christ, by whom the world is crucified unto me, and I unto the world. And as many as walk according to this rule, peace be on them, and mercy, and upon the Israel of God" (Gal. 6:14, 16).

Pride of self is the door to "paradise lost." Sacrifice of self is the door to "paradise regained." The assertion of self-pride brought the first banishment from God's presence. "How art thou fallen from heaven, O Lucifer, son of the morning! . . . For thou hast said in thine heart, . . . I will exalt my throne above the stars of God" (Isa. 14:12–13).

The second banishment from God's presence and from the Garden of Eden came also as the result of a desire to be as God. Satan was acquainted with the tremendous appeal of self-pride, for it had caused his own defeat. It is still his lethal weapon when all other methods fail. How common it is to see one sacrifice the gain and the good of a lifetime in order that self might remain on the pedestal!

God has made available to man a greater power than that of self, a power which will enable him to break these chains of slavery which he has forged about himself.

In the state of Kentucky there is a tree that retains its leaves throughout the winter storms. The sting of freezing weather and the blasts of winter winds leave it undaunted as it seems to boast its power of holding its leaves. Then the springtime tells a different story. The rising of the sap with its gentle flow out into the limbs and twigs pushes the leaves from their winter anchorage and accomplishes that which the winter storms had failed to do.

One power only is able to dethrone self in man. "Now abideth faith, hope, charity [love], these three; but the greatest of these is charity [*love*]" (1 Cor. 13:13). Our Lord himself stated that the goal to which all the law and the prophets would lead man could be attained through love, for only through love shall all the law and the prophets be fulfilled. Man's love must extend in two directions. The first is man's love as it reaches back to him who died on the cross. The second is man's love reaching out to his fellowman. A love of man for both God and his fellowman, when great enough, has never failed to bring man to the *second cross*.

Again we say, God's will for man in his world is *peace*, but it can only come when man so loves as God so loved.

All varnish put on love immediately becomes transparent. If love is present, it will not be hidden. If love is absent, no veneer can cover this fact. A gift or deed not made in love is like the gift of a dollar after devaluation. We citizens of the United States might well ask why our nation has given more than any other nation in history and yet is hated even by those who accept our gifts. The answer can be found largely in the lack of love accompanying our gifts. A man bringing a gift in a condescending manner can only repel, not win friends. To make a gift in love the giver must step down from his pedestal. Rarely have citizens of the United States, whether tourists or ambassadors, given up their pedestal. Perhaps James Russell Lowell's words were meant for this hour. "He who gives himself feeds three: himself, his hungry neighbor, and me."

The answer to peace in the world, and among men, can and must come only through the two crosses, to which the

Master himself came to show men the way. "Who, being in the form of God, thought it not robbery to be equal with God: but made himself of no reputation, and took upon him the form of a servant, and was made in the likeness of men: and being found in fashion as a man, he humbled himself, and became obedient unto death, even the death of the cross" (Phil. 2:6–8).

As our Lord walked into Jerusalem for the last time, knowing a cross awaited him, he also pointed to a second cross that awaited all who would follow him. He pointed to both crosses when he said, "The hour is come, that the Son of man should be glorified. Verily, verily, I say unto you, except a corn of wheat fall into the ground and die, it abideth alone: but if it die, it bringeth forth much fruit. He that loveth his life shall lose it, and he that hateth his life in this world shall keep it unto life eternal. If any man serve me, let him follow me" (John 12:23–26). To "follow me" will bring him also to a cross.

Two crosses Paul also found he must accept—that of Christ and his own, for he wrote: "I am crucified with Christ: nevertheless I live; yet not I, but Christ liveth in me: and the life which I now live in the flesh I live by the faith of the Son of God, who loved me, and gave himself for me" (Gal. 2:20).

Two crosses span the gulf between God and the world. But through the acceptance of the two crosses by both God and man, peace will come on earth. And the message of the angels that heralded his birth, On earth "Peace, good will among men" will prove to have been neither an idle boast of the angels nor a goal beyond the reach of man.

17.

The Church Facing Tomorrow
Without Spirit-filled Men

The catalyst in this book is the word "second"—the second cross, the second land, and the second love. This book would not need to have been written if men would follow the first and greatest commandment and the second which is like unto it, "Thou shalt love thy neighbor as thyself." The church that is to serve tomorrow, and to which men shall again make a well-beaten path, must return to the priorities as given by our Lord—the two crosses.

The storms shall not endanger the church that is anchored to two crosses over, which are emblazoned the one word "love." Over the first cross man must be able to read: Here God so loved. Over the second he must be able to read: Here is the place the followers of Christ so loved. If the Christian today is to follow our Lord as a disciple, he, too, shall surely come to a cross for the crucifixion of self. When anchored to those two crosses the church has withstood through the ages every attack made upon it and will again triumph as it faces the most serious tests of tomorrow.

In its two crosses alone the church has found, and will find, strength. Our Lord surely was thinking of the survival of the church when he gave the disciples the unfailing formula for survival, a formula that combines the two most powerful elements in the universe: "God so loved" and "I command you that you love one another as I have loved you."

Not until many churches are willing to replace the man-made commandments which they attempt to impose on men with the divine commandments which alone can meet the needs of men will those churches deserve the preeminence which our Lord gave to his church.

It is not true that the church needs to face the uncertain future with no adequate message for the hour. It is not true that the church has no foundation to which it can point men and say, "Build here." This foundation will not fail. The message of Paul, "Love never faileth," has never been more true, more needed, or even more adequate for any age than our own. The churches will meet and will continue to meet the needs of this age only in proportion to their faithfulness in proclaiming and persuading men to accept the two crosses. Without Christ's cross the church has no hope for a lost world. Without the second cross there is no channel for that message to the world. "By this shall all men know that ye are my disciples, if ye have love one for another" (John 13:35). "Love one another, as I have loved you" (John 15:12). Our Lord could well have added, "I speak of a love great enough to take you too to a cross."

This world needs a message from God, and God will give it to the world, even if he has to give it outside some established churches. Without him the church simply becomes another institution providing thrones for men instead of crosses and creating masters instead of servants.

As we said in the introduction, the church, or the Christian, that loses the anchor to either cross becomes no more meaningful or helpful than a globe that has become detached at one end and hangs at a crazy angle. Both offer only a perverted view. Neither offers help to him who comes seeking guidance for the journey ahead.

The church has been weakened today by pet plans and projects being given priority over the two crosses. These priorities have not been given by labeling them as number one and number two, but by the dethronement of the gospel of our Lord preached and the enthronement of pet projects and priorities. The majors in the New Testament church have too often become the minors in the present-day churches. These minors are so often and so fervently proclaimed from the pulpit that the casual observer would find it difficult to believe: that the first and greatest commandment given the church was to love God and the second was like unto it, to love your fellowman. On the basis of time alone given to certain projects in the church one could only conclude that to attend some particular meeting was far more important than to love one's fellowman.

The activities in many churches today would convince the one outside looking in that the pet projects or doctrines of that particular church are more important to its members than the two crosses, or the two loves, or to another experience to which the Holy Spirit would lead every Christian. Before 1492 the motto of Spain's flag was *ne plus ultra* (nothing beyond). After Columbus discovered a new world the motto was shortened to *plus ultra* (more beyond). This also is the call to today's Christian—more beyond!